JOURNEY to the BIG WORLD

Revision of DARE to TAKE the NEXT STEP

By Frank Hegyi

For partial financial support

Published by

Frank Hegyi Publications

1240 Kilborn Place, Unit 5

Ottawa, Ontario

Canada K1H 1B4

www.hegyipublications.com

© Frank Hegyi – 2008

Revised: @Frank Hegyi - 2014

ISBN 978-0-9812495-0-6

All rights reserved

Contents

ACKNOWLEDGEMENT 5

INTRODUCTION 7

GROWING UP IN THE WAR ZONE 9

LIFE UNDER COMMUNISM 21

FREEDOM FIGHTER 41

RE-BUILDING A SHATTERED LIFE 59

INTO THE AMAZON RAIN FORESTS 89

INTEGRATING INTO CANADA 101

RETURN TO THE OLD COUNTRY 125

TO SUCCEED PROFESSIONALLY 137

VISIT TO THE SOVIET UNION 149

INTERNATIONAL ADVENTURES 165

VOLUNTEERING TO REPAY SOCIETY 179

JOINING THE PRIVATE SECTOR 193

CONCLUSION 207

Journey to the Big World

Acknowledgement

As a young boy, I used to sit on the knee of my grandfather (Nagy Papa) and listen to his many stories about the *big world*. Grandfather never travelled further than about 100 km from the village. He had never seen a movie, but he had read a few books, including the Bible. He used to read the newspaper every day and sometimes the fancy color magazines that had pictures in them about major cities, especially Vienna. His vision of the *big world* evolved from these pictures.

Not surprisingly, inspired by Nagy Papa, at the age of three, when my mother scolded me, I packed some food in a basket and started out on my journey to the *big world*. Our village priest, who was an amateur photographer and always had his camera with him, saw me when I was coming out of our house and asked where I was going. I told him I was to go to see the *big world*.

I dedicate this book to Nagy Papa.

Journey to the Big World

Introduction

This is a revised version of the first edition: *Dare to Take the Next Step*. Some of the sections are taken out and referenced in other books. Specifically, the sections are:

- Part of the South American section is included in The Stroke book; and
- My cancer is referenced in the Death Can Wait version.

This book is dedicated to my grandfather who told me many stories about the *big world*.

Journey to the Big World

Growing up in the War Zone

Near the end of the Second World War, we lived in western Hungary where the fighting between the Red Army and German soldiers was from door-to-door. While the front moved back and forth, we were hiding in an underground bunker. When the Germans were in control of our village, a couple of the soldiers came into our house to warm up in the evening.

I was six years old and remember sitting on the knee of one of the soldiers called Hans while he was singing for me in German a song that he really wanted to sing for his son who was the same age as I. Hans spoke a little bit of Hungarian and was telling my parents that, although he had been away from his family for a long time, he hoped to see his son and wife soon.

After one of the door-to-door fighting escapades between German and Russian soldiers, we were returning to our house from the bunker where we had sought shelter and we saw Hans lying there not moving. He was covered with blood.

Grandfather said with anger, "Damn Hitler, damn Stalin, damn the war."

We had been a happy family before the war came to our village. My parents had a small farm that produced rye, wheat, potatoes, cabbage, and corn. The farm also included a couple of parcels of pasture. At the back of the house, we had fruit trees and, in the summer time, we had lots of apples, apricots, prunes, cherries, walnuts and pears. Our house was big enough to have a separate bedroom where all five of us slept. There was also a kitchen with a wooden stove and large table, a storage room for food and, at the back of the house, there was a stable for the cows and horses. A barn kept the food for the animals.

My parents worked long hours on the farm, planting the crops, hoeing the potato and corn fields, and harvesting at the end of the summer. They didn't have much time to spend with me so I became very close to my grandfather who was always there. We spent a lot of time minding the cows as they were grazing on the pastures and grandfather always had new stories to tell me about the world beyond our little village. He was very popular in the village as a storyteller and, on Sunday afternoons, some of my friends used to come to our house to listen to his many exciting stories. I enjoyed his stories so much that I wanted to see the *big world* for myself.

One day I set out to explore the *big world*. I packed some food in a basket and left home. I was nearly three years old and ready for the adventure. I wasn't too far from our house when I met Father Lenarsics, the village priest and amateur photographer, who took the picture displayed in the front of the book.

After this, my mother started to spent more time with me and often came out from the kitchen to the porch where grandfather had a special chair and I used to sit on his knee while he was telling stories. My mother seemed to like the stories because she often asked him, "What happened next?"

Picture 1. My Mother and I.

Picture 2. My father and I.

Picture 3. The house in which I was born.

As I was growing up, an important job in the village was grazing cows in the meadows and in the nearby forest. Grandfather and I were given this job and we enjoyed it very much. He used to hide a piece of bread in one of his pockets, which he saved for me because he knew that I would get hungry after a few hours being out in the fresh air. He enjoyed watching me as I was trying to find the bread without being too obvious that I was looking for it. We sat for hours under the trees as he told me fascinating stories, always about the *big world* (nagyvilág). When he saw pictures in a magazine of the nobility in Vienna, he made up so many stories for me about how they lived, the type of horse carriage they traveled in and the delicious food that they would eat.

The stories took us over the ocean (the *big water*) to lands that had large fields for the cows to graze on. He called that land: America. When I asked grandfather if we could go together to see the *big world*, he would smile under his bushy moustache, and say, "Only in our dreams".

On Sunday mornings, we all went to the Roman Catholic Church for the 11 o'clock Mass. That was the time when village people would show off their Sunday best. Father Lenarsics always had interesting stories from the Bible and we were scared when he was describing hell, a place that we would end up if we didn't behave the way that he was telling us to live.

After Mass, people stood around just outside the church, exchanging stories about their work on the farms, as well as spreading some gossip about couples who started to date or about young lads who got drunk the night before. We children would always listen to these stories until someone shouted at us to go and play somewhere else.

My mother made sure that I went to church every Sunday, attended catechism lessons on Saturday morning and served as an altar boy. Father Lenarsics took special notice of my participation in catechism classes and of being an altar boy and told my mother that I should study to be a priest. I was so excited when my mother sat down beside me and told me what Father Lenarsics said to her.

I eagerly replied, "Yes, Mother. I will become a priest when I grow up." I could hardly wait for the time when my father would come home from the fields and I could tell him what I wanted to be when I grow up. As it turned out, Father was not happy with this news because he said that he wanted me to be a farmer just like him. He also asked me if I knew why priests always wear a long black skirt.

I said, "I don't know. Why?"

He said, "Because priests have to get their wee-wee cut off. That is why they always wear that long black skirt." Father always knew everything best, so I believed him.

Unfortunately for my father, I asked the priest next time he visited us, "Did they really cut off your wee-wee?" That night my father slept in the barn and he had to go to confession the following Sunday.

Then our peaceful little world was gradually shaken up by the war.

First, we saw the SS soldiers and Hungarian police taking the Rosenthal family into a truck on a Sunday as we were coming out of church. Mr. Rosenthal owned the shop where I used to buy candies. He used to give me an extra one and was always nice to me and called me Ferike. They hit them with their rifles as they were dragged from their home.

I saw his son, who was also called Ferike, run after his Daddy, crying, "Papa, Papa, I love you."

Mr. Rosenthal picked up Ferike. I saw him crying, too. One of the soldiers hit Mr. Rosenthal in the stomach with his rifle as he fell into the truck still holding his son.

I asked my father, "Why are the soldiers taking the Rosenthal's away from their home?"

Father answered sadly, "Because they are Jews and the SS are very bad. The Nazi's are taking Jewish people into concentration camps and killing them."

Soon after the Rosenthal family was taken away, we saw German soldiers marching through our village. They were recruiting some of the lads in the village to join them. One of the families in the village was very poor. They did not have warm jackets and boots during the winter. Two of their sons joined up and were bragging about the nice clothes they were given by the Germans.

Near the end of the war, our village was occupied by German soldiers. I still remember the SS marching through the main street while we were hiding behind the window. The soldiers came into our house and my father was taken away, along with other men, to dig trenches as the front was retreating from Russia through Hungary. We did not see my father for a month. One night he returned, having managed to escape as the shooting escalated between the German and Russian soldiers. He told us that the front was expected to reach our village at any time and we had to prepare for it.

The next morning my father, grandfather and mother started to dig in the backyard, making a bunker for us to hide in. It was a hole in the ground, about eight feet by eight feet by eight feet, with about two feet of hay on the floor. At one end, they made steps so we could go into it. They placed wooden planks on top and covered it with soil from the garden to make it look like a large flower bed. The entrance was covered with hay so nobody would suspect that it was a bunker.

The fighting reached our village by evening, so my parents, grandfather and I took food and warm blankets with us to the bunker. At night, we heard soldiers running outside, shouting in German, then in Russian. The fighting lasted for over a week as our village changed hands several times. When the fighting appeared to have stopped, my father took me back to the house to get more supplies. My grandfather stayed with my mother in the bunker to protect her in case some of the soldiers discovered our hiding place.

As my father and I were returning from the house, the shooting started again, soldiers were chasing each other. A low flying British plane was spraying machine gun bullets at the side of our house. My father picked me up and ran with me as bullets were hitting the ground. Miraculously, we made it back to the bunker without even an injury.

On April 4th 1945, Hungary was officially *liberated* by the Red Army and life returned slowly to a peaceful level. However, people in the village were still afraid of Russian soldiers who often went on a looting binge after drinking too much vodka. At such times, my father would hide my mother in a shed that housed the ducks in order to protect her from drunken Russian soldiers.

My father was very angry with the politics that were developing after the Second World War. I remember when I entered Grade 6 in September 1949 and came home with the red tie of the pioneers, he wanted to burn it. My grandfather had to explain to him that the students had no choice but to become members of the young Communist group and if Father burned the tie, they would put him in jail.

One of my friends in school drew a moustache on the picture of the Communist leader, Mátyás Rákosi and he was severely punished by the principal. The police took his father away for a month. When his father came home, he was very quiet. My friend told us that his father had been beaten many times by the police. After that we were scared of the police, especially the AVH whom the people in the village called the Secret Police.

My father asked me not to repeat to anyone what I might hear at home about government officials or the police. He was worried that he, too, might be taken away and beaten up. He also called a family meeting with doors and windows locked and told us that his younger brother, István, was accused of being sympathetic to Tito. When Rajk was executed, István escaped to Yugoslavia, fearful that the Rákosi group might imprison him. Unfortunately for István, the Yugoslav border guards loyal to Moscow handed him back. István was tortured by AVH first in Szombathely and then in Budapest where the AVH had its headquarters. After that, István was taken to Recsk, the death camp set up by the AVH for political prisoners.

Our family was very scared of what might to happen to us. I was in Grade School and our principal was a strong Communist. Father told us to be very careful who we talked to and to make sure that we never criticized the Communist leaders and what they were doing. We heard rumors about other families who were declared reactionaries. Many had been Communist deported to the lowlands. With one uncle interned at Recsk and another uncle working as a police officer in the Horthy Regime, Father was worried that we might be targeted for deportation. After that, we lived in fear on a day-to-day basis, awaiting the possibility of deportation.

In school, we marched on April 4th (Liberation Day) and on May Day and were lead by the school principal chanting, *Tito mérges kigyó* (poisonous snake). At that time we did not understand why we had to hate Toto and the Yugoslav people.

My father was very attached to the land that he inherited from my grandfather. The total area of our farm was around thirty-five hectares. In 1952, we had the best harvest on the land. There was enough rye, wheat, barley, corn, sugar beets and potatoes for us to live comfortably until the next harvest. My father planned to sell some of the produce at the nearby market to get some money so we could buy much needed clothes and household items that our farm didn't produce. As soon as we completed the harvest, however, the local Communists came to our house and told Father that he must join the collective farm. Father was very stubborn and refused. My mother begged him to do as they asked, but he refused. Shortly after that, one of the local Communists was watching our house. She started to issue heavy fines for anything, including one of our cows dropping feces on the road outside of our house or the family dog barking too loud. The list of infractions was endless and pointless. Father finally gave in to Communist demands, but by that time we had lost most of the food supply for the winter.

In June 1952, I finished Grade 8 and was hoping to go to Gimnázium (High School). My father's resistance to join the collective farm and my uncle's imprisonment prevented that wish. I was refused admission to High School and was told to sign up as a laborer in the local collective farm.

Journey to the Big World

By the time winter came, our food supply was mostly gone. Father worked in the stables of the collective farm, looking after cows. He was able to bring home milk every day, but was not going to get paid until the next year's harvest. The Communists broke his spirit as he was not able to provide for his family. He was always a very proud man, a little bit on the stubborn side. Seeing his family hungry put him into deep depression. One night as we watched my seven year old sister crying herself to sleep because she was hungry, my hatred towards the Communists intensified. I vowed for revenge at the right opportunity. Now, I had to focus on helping our family to survive.

The next day I went to the collective farm and asked the chairman how I could earn money to buy food for our family. He said that the collective farm needed acorns to feed the pigs. I went home and Mother and I walked in the snow for three kilometers to the nearest forest which had oak trees that produced the acorns. We could not afford to buy gloves. Instead, we used a piece of rag to cover our hands as we cleared the snow to find the acorns. We each filled the sack half full and then carried it on our heads back to the village. This gave us some cash to buy food. Once a week, I went on the bicycle to the next town called Sárvár, which was ten kilometers from our village, and stood in line for up to two hours to buy a loaf of bread. Bread and milk was our steady diet and occasionally my mother would kill a chicken on Sunday to provide a more complete meal such as chicken Paprikás.

Before Father was forced to join the collective farm, we had a vineyard that produced a good crop of grapes, yielding five

Journey to the Big World

barrels of wine each containing about 150 liters. Father reopened the hidden cellar in the barn that we used to hide wine from Russian soldiers. We lowered the barrels into the cellar with heavy ropes then covered them with wooden planks and hay.

We were fortunate that the Communists never discovered this family treasure. By December 1952, the wine had fermented enough and was drinkable. Mother and I took about ten liters of this wine to the nearest town and sold it to people that we knew, knowing that they would not report us to the police. Selling wine on the black market was illegal and if we were caught we both would have ended up in jail. Proceeds from the wine sales helped the family to buy some basic groceries from the village store.

Grandfather also collected apples, prunes and other fruit that were under the trees each fall. He put them in barrels and covered it with earth. In the winter, Grandfather and I put a barrel on a sled around midnight and pulled it over five kilometers into the forest where there was an illegal distillery. We went back to get the rest of the barrels during the next three nights, then we were ready to produce pálinka (a kind of prunes brandy which looks like vodka). The barrels of fallen fruit gave us a good supply of pálinka which we transported back to our house the next night.

My mother and I would take a couple of bottles into town once a week and sell it on the black market. This helped to provide easier cash than collecting acorns from under the snow. The cash provided the means to buy food.

Life under Communism

During World War II, a Communist cell headed by László Rajk a veteran of the Spanish Civil War and a former student Communist leader, operated underground within Hungary. Mátyás Rákosi led a second cell from Moscow. After the Soviet Red Army invaded Hungary in September 1944, Rajk's organization emerged from hiding and the Rákosi group returned to Hungary. Rákosi's close ties with the Soviets enhanced his influence within the party, and a rivalry developed between the Muscovites and Rajk's followers.

In 1942, Rákosi became a leading politician among the Hungarian Communists. Rákosi returned to Hungary on January 30, 1945, when the Soviet leadership sent him to Debrecen, the provisional seat of government, to organize the Communist party. On February 22, 1945, Rákosi became General Secretary of the Central Committee of the Hungarian Communist Party.[1]

Rákosi described himself as "Stalin's best Hungarian disciple" and "Stalin's best pupil." He also invented the term *salami tactics*, which related to his tactic of eliminating the opposition slice by slice. Under Rákosi, an imitator of Stalinist

---

[1] *Mátyás Rákosi (1892-1971)*

http://www.rev.hu/history_of_56/szerviz/kislex/biograf/rakosi.htm .

political and economic programs, Hungary experienced one of the harshest dictatorships in Europe

From May to November 1945, Rajk was Secretary of the Hungarian Communist Party Budapest Committee, and from then until March 1946, Deputy General Secretary of the Hungarian Communist Party.

As Minister of Interior, Rajk organized the Hungarian Communist Party's private army and the brutal Secret Police (an organization analogous to the SS and KGB). Under the cover of "struggle against fascism and reaction" and "defense of the power of proletariat", he prohibited and liquidated several religious, national, democratic and maverick establishments and groups (the number of these was about 1500).

In September 1948 János Kádár became the Minister of Interior who expanded further the scope of the Secret Police under another new name AVH (Állam Védelmi Hatóság or State Protection Agency). Born in Fiume (now Rijeka, Croatia), Kádár spent his first six years with foster parents until reunited with his mother who sent him to school until he was fourteen. He apprenticed as a typewriter mechanic, joined the trade union's youth group at seventeen, and joined the illegal Hungarian Communist Party in 1931. Kádár was subsequently arrested several times for unlawful political activities. He was sentenced for two years imprisonment in 1933.

In 1946, Kádár was elected Deputy Secretary-General of the Hungarian Communist Party. In 1949, he succeeded Rajk as Minister of the Interior.[2]

Kádár greatly expanded the mandate of AVH to include patrolling the borders, waterways, and airways, supervising the movements of foreigners, and controlling the issuance of passports and visas. The network of 40,000 secret agents covered the entire country and compiled documentation on approximately 1.8 million (18 % of the population) citizens who were "considered" security risks. This rapid expansion was made possible because Gábor Péter took his orders directly from Rákosi.

Rákosi orchestrated Rajk's show trial mainly to please Stalin who was furious with Marshall Tito. Rákosi asked Stalin about the punishment that Rajk should receive. Initially, Stalin suggested life imprisonment, but two days later recommended the death sentence. Rajk was to be made an example for the beginning of Stalin's anti-Titoist purges. Rajk, along with Dr Tibor Szönyi and András Szalai, was sentenced to death by hanging.

Kádár watched the hanging from a window overlooking the prison yard with Péter and Mihály Farkas (Minister of Defense). When it was over, they toasted with pálinka (prunes brandy) the AVH officer who obtained the false confession from Rajk through physical and mental torture.

---

[2] http://en.wikipedia.org/wiki/J%C3%A1nos_K%C3%A1d%C3%A1r

Rákosi strongly promoted the Soviet collectivization model which was introduced by Stalin in the late 1920s as a way to boost agricultural production through the organization of land and labor into collectives called collective farms (kolkhozes). In July 1948, government regulations allowed the seizure of larger landholdings from *nagygazdák* (Hungarian *kulaks*), who owned land that was larger than fifty-seven hectares. This legislation redistributed 35% of Hungary's territory, some 93,000 square kilometers of land.

With the opposition parties disbanded and the trade unions becoming ineffective, the churches became the Communists' main source of opposition. The government had expropriated the churches' property with the land reform, and, in July 1948, it nationalized church schools. Protestant church leaders reached a compromise with the government, but the head of the Roman Catholic Church, Cardinal Jozsef Mindszenty, resisted. He was arrested on December 26, 1948.

In August 1952 Rákosi became Prime Minister of Hungary. His authoritarian dictatorship had no limits. Under his orders, AVH jailed and tortured thousands of Communists who appeared to be a threat to the *bald murderer and dictator*. Under Rákosi and Communist rule, secularism and not religion was favored and Zionism and Jewish observance were outlawed, and many Jews were expelled from the cities to the provinces for a time. Rákosi's attack on the Jews was prompted by the anti-Semitic developments that were unfolding in the Soviet Union.

On January 3, 1953 Péter was arrested as a backlash of the Jewish Doctor's show trial in the Soviet Union because Péter was also of Jewish descent (although he did not practice his religion). This in fact happened on Rákosi's order to show loyalty to Stalin who was also displaying anti-Semitic tendencies. High ranking Communists welcomed this development because they never knew when Péter would order their own internment and torture.

On March 5, 1953 the soviet dictator, Stalin, died. The news and circumstances of his death made Rákosi nervous. Reliable reports indicated that on March 1, 1953, after an all-night dinner with Interior Minister Beria and other high ranking Communist leaders including Malenkov, Bulganin and Khrushchev, Stalin did not emerge from his room. It was determined that he had probably suffered a stroke that paralyzed the right side of his body. Strangely, the guards were under orders not to disturb him and he was not discovered until that evening. It has been suggested that Stalin was poisoned and all indications pointed to Beria, chief of the Soviet security and police apparatus.

In Eastern Europe, the new spirit evident in the Kremlin caused concern among the various mini-Stalins who held power. In June 1953, Rákosi and other party leaders were summoned to Moscow, where Soviet leaders harshly criticized them for Hungary's dismal economic performance. Rákosi retained his position as party chief, but the Soviet leaders forced the appointment of Nagy as prime minister. He quickly won the support of the government ministries and the intelligentsia. Nagy also ended the purges and began freeing political prisoners from the forced labour camps.

In his first address to the National Assembly as Prime Minister, Nagy attacked Rákosi for his use of terror, and the speech was printed in the party newspaper. Nagy charted his *New Course* for Hungary's drifting economy in a speech before the Central Committee, which gave the plan unanimous approval.

The most important measures of the New Course concerned restraining the excessive coercion of the authorities and relieving the oppression that weighed on the people. The amnesty measures that were taken fell into four main groups. First, large numbers of people were released from confinement, excused from paying fines, or relieved of various legal disabilities that resulted from having a criminal record. Secondly, the government abolished several types of sentences and penal institutions used in recent years. The forced labor camps were closed and sentences such as internal exile and designation of a compulsory place of residence were dropped.

Although the New Course had brought several important results by the autumn of 1954, the steps taken had not led to a breakthrough in any field. In each case, the group behind Rákosi had successfully attacked and weakened the reforms. This meant that Nagy's policies did nothing to satisfy those in Moscow who had demanded the changes. Unfortunately the outcome of the changes was greater turmoil, not the order that Moscow sought.

It became clear that Nagy's ideas differed substantially from the role in which Moscow had cast him in 1953. The Kremlin had wanted the changes to bring peace and calm to Hungary, while Nagy was aiming at a real reform of Socialism and of the building of Socialism.

By the spring of 1953, people in our village had adjusted gradually to the lifestyle of the collective farms. Even my father abandoned his resistance to the local Communists and started to fit in to the new conditions. He was a very good farmer, had an excellent knowledge of crop rotation and knew how to look after the animals on the farm. He was appointed leader of the brigade that looked after the few hundred cows in the collective farm.

The leaders of the collective farms were not skilled farmers. Many of these leaders were only *promoted* because they had joined the Communist party and were loyal to the Soviet style agricultural practices. Similarly, the President of the Village Council, János Mosonyi, had no administrative skills in running the affairs of the village. Previously, Mosonyi had worked as a laborer, pushing a wheel barrel on the main roads, filling fill the holes in the road with gravel and earth. He had a Grade 6 education.

In 1949, Mosonyi joined the Communist party and was *promoted* to the powerful position of President, Village Council. The notary public who was a High School graduate and previously was the administrator of the village did all the work and János' job was to sign all papers dealing with the affairs of the village and to listen to the comments of villagers in order to ensure that nobody would criticize the Communist leadership. Whenever somebody made an inappropriate comment, János would pass that information to the police and such a person would be dealt with by the Secret Police. The punishment usually was a few weeks in jail and beatings until the person would confess his sins and promise not to do it again.

On Friday, March 6, 1953, I was working as a laborer on the collective farm in a woodlot which was about four kilometers from our village. Around noon, one of the supervisors of the collective farm came to our brigade riding a horse and asked us to listen to an announcement.

"Comrades," he said. "I have very sad news. It is with deep sadness that I am announcing the passing of Comrade Stalin."

We were then asked to observe a minute of silence. I had to be careful not to show my desire to smile after hearing the good news.

After Stalin's death, the suppression of people by the Communists eased. We were all taken back with the changes that occurred when Nagy replaced Rákosi as Prime Minister. He freed the political prisoners, including my Uncle István. When Uncle István came home from the labour camp in Recsk, the family huddled up behind closed doors to hear what happened to him. We could hardly believe that human beings could be that cruel. He was severely beaten daily when he was at the AVH holding cell in Szombathely. When he was interned at the AVH headquarters in Budapest, the same place where Cardinal Mindszenty was interned (60 Andrássy ut), the real cruelty reached unbelievable heights.

Uncle István described the tortures he received in the basement cells at the AVH headquarters. He spent nights barefooted in a cell that was full of running water and rats. The cruelty included:

➢ Beatings with rubber batons until he became unconscious;

➢ Two or three policemen kicking him with boots when he was tackled down to the floor until he passed out;

➤ Standing naked in a small cell and if he leaned against a wall, he would receive a painful electric shock;

➤ Shoving salt into his mouth then being forced to drink water from the toilet bowl;

➤ Going without food for days;

➤ Going without sleep for many nights and days;

➤ Being handcuffed and in leg irons for several days and nights.

Fellow prisoners included former Communist leaders, intellectuals, writers, farmers, labourers and priests. The guards used to brag about the treatment that was especially designed by Rákosi for priests. After sever beatings, a priest would be given a crucifix to kiss. Unbeknownst to the priest, the crucifix would be charged with electricity and sometimes the dose was large enough to electrocute the priest.

The torture was to obtain a false confession to confirm that he was an agent of the foreign Imperialists and Tito. When he could not take the pain anymore, then he signed a confession that he could not even read because his eyes were too swollen from the beatings. He was then taken to the labour camp at Recsk which was also known as a death camp. There, the purpose was to torture prisoners on a continuous basis. He said the first day he was taken outside to work in below freezing temperatures and when he tripped and fell in the snow in from of one of the guards, the guard stepped on his bare hands with his spiked boots and twisted his leg until blood was pouring out of his hand. He had to tear off a piece from his shirt to bandage the hand so that he could continue working without gloves.

Uncle István told us how determined he was to survive, even though the AVH guards kept telling him that he was in a death camp. They would say, "You are here to suffer and die as soon as you are too weak to work." He struggled on a daily basis to keep up his strength. Besides working in the quarry, my uncle did push ups and other exercises. When he came home, he could no longer fit into the riding boots that he had worn before his internment. His leg muscles had increased the breadth of the calves of his legs.

As we listened to Uncle István (Pista Bácsi), my anger at the Communists increased. I could not understand how anyone could be that cruel and inhumane to another human being. That feeling of wanting revenge came back again, but I knew that the time was not right.

In July 1953, I begged my father to let me go to High School. My mother leant her support in my request. My grandfather also argued on my behalf, pointing out to Father that I should not have to spend the rest of my life on the collective farm as a labourer. The main source of my father's resistance was that his younger brother went to High School and yet he still ended up in the death camp.

I pointed out to Father, "Now that Uncle István is free and that you are a respected worker in the collective farm, they should let me go to High School."

After some discussion my father gave in to our pressure and accompanied me to the High School in Sárvár. In the new political climate, the principal was very cooperative and registered me right away to enter into first year. I was extremely happy with this turn of events.

During the rest of the summer, I picked fruit from the trees in our backyard. Early each morning, I would put one basket full on the back of the bicycle and another two on each side on the handle bar and bike to the market in Sárvár where I would sell the apples, cherries, peaches, apricots and plums to raise some money for school books and cloths. Several of the older women who were regular merchants took a liking to me and gave big smiles as I was trying to attract customers. When I had fruit left over, I would sell it to these ladies at half price and they would make a profit on the produce the next morning. By September, I was ready to start High School. The ordeal of working on the collective farm was over.

In March 1954, my father came home from the collective farm with the news that he could take our land out of the collective farm and continue working it as an independent farmer. My mother and father discussed this option with grandfather while we children listened. Father had lost interest in owning the farm again. The working cows were gone; there was no grain to put in the ground; and, what finally swayed the decision, was that he did not trust the Communists. "What if they change their mind again in a year or so, what then?" he pondered out loud. He remained in the collective farm.

I enjoyed studying in the High School and even started to write poetry. Sárvár was ten kilometres from our village. I rode my bicycle to school every day. In the fall, I would spend a couple of hours at the market in the morning selling fruit then went to school. In the evening, I studied at home beside the window. When the sun went down, I lit a lantern to continue with the homework. There was electricity in Sárvár, but it still had not reached our village.

Writing poetry offered me refuge from the political turmoil that was still going on in Hungary. Father was quite a philosopher and always had an interesting way of describing the politically dominated lifestyle. He used to say, "Son, be careful. Under Communism, the higher you climb up on the ladder, the bigger the fall in the end."

During the winter, I joined an amateur theatre group and landed the leading part in a play called, *Gypsy Blacksmith*. It was quite a hit in the village and many people came up to me saying, "You look just like your grandfather."

I was starting to demonstrate an interest in history at school. Our text books were full of praises for the Soviet Union and Hungarian history was re-written by the Communists, saying that everything was wrong with previous Regimes and the Communist system was the only one which cared for the working class. I found this line hard to swallow especially in the light of what they had done to my father and uncle. While I loved my father very much, I did not agree with him on some of the decisions he had made concerning his battle with the Regime. Once again, I turned to my grandfather, trying to find the answers.

Grandfather told me, "You are Hegyi and come from a line where every second generation tried to do something better than the previous one."

I asked grandfather to tell me a little bit of our family's history. He gladly obliged. Grandfather was very proud of our family's origin he was able to trace it back to 1847, when the Hegyi's were members of the Hungarian nobility.

"Our family," Grandfather related our story, "owned a substantial amount of land near the Austrian border, including a village. Tragedy struck the family in 1847 when my grandmother died giving birth to a boy, her firstborn. The housekeeper of the estate, who had also given birth to a baby just a few weeks prior to this tragedy, cared for the young infant. In 1848, my grandfather joined the revolution against the Habsburg Empire. He died in battle and the land was taken away by greedy relatives without making provisions for the orphan Hegyi boy.

"My father was brought up as a servant by the former housekeeper and worked all of his life as a farm labourer. I was born in the servant's quarters of the former Hegyi Estate in 1870. After finishing Grade 4 in school, I worked as a farm labourer and by the time I was twenty-years-old, I became an entrepreneur by bidding on jobs in neighbouring estates to supply labourers for hoeing potato and corn fields, harvesting crops such as wheat, rye and barley, and picking apples and plums in fruit orchards. At age twenty-four, I went to a dance in a nearby village called Szemegye and I asked a beautiful young girl, Anna Vajkovics, for a csardas (a fast Hungarian folk dance).

"I was a tall (over six feet) handsome man (or so I was often told) with a typical bushy moustache. I wore black riding boots which were fashionable at the time. Anna complimented me on my dancing. That encouraged me to ask her for the next dance...again and again, until they played the last slow waltz. I asked permission to accompany Anna to the front gate of her home." He winked at me. "That way I was able to find out where she lived.

"The next Sunday afternoon, I, still wearing his Sunday best suit that was reserved mainly for church, rode my bicycle to make a call at Anna's house. I think Anna was kind of hoping that I would call on her because she was still in her church-going dress at three in the afternoon! The Sunday visits became regular and two years later, I asked Anna's father for her hand in marriage. Since my business was expanding to nearby villages, and Anna's parents were getting on in age, the two of them decided to live in the Vajkovics home in Szemegye."

Grandfather always talked affectionately about Grandmother. He always described her beautiful smile, how well she danced and the dream they had about having their own land and a large family. They both shared an entrepreneurial spirit and the desire to buy land that they could call their own. Grandmother was an excellent cook and according to Grandfather, she made the best pork schnitzel and pork goulash with nokedli (spaetzel) that he ever tasted.

One evening, when Grandfather paid his many complements for the good meal, Grandmother suggested that they could earn extra money by feeding the contract farm workers, many of whom were single men and would welcome a good home cooked meal. Initially, they started feeding just a few laborers who worked on nearby farms, but the business expanded fast as the reputation of my grandmother's cooking spread to other workers. Since Grandmother always made sure that everyone had a good meal, she usually cooked a little bit more than the men could eat.

Grandfather came up with the idea of raising pigs on the leftover food. This venture became highly profitable because now they had to buy less pork to feed the men. In less than ten years, they saved up enough to buy a farm of their own. Grandmother had a brother in Nyögér so the two of them got took a horse-drawn carriage to make a visit to this upland village and look for land to purchase.

Luck was on their side as a thirty-four-hectare and highly fertile land was up for sale after the death of the owner. The land came with a nice house on the main street which had a large backyard, a stable for ten animals and a barn. They had enough savings to pay for this farm in cash and, according to Grandfather, they even had money left over to buy another horse and four dairy cows. So, in 1906 my grandparents moved to Nyögér. They already had an eight-year-old daughter, Maria, a six-year-old son, Antal, and a two-year-old son, Ferenc (my father). In 1908, they had a daughter whom they named, Margit, and another girl, Emi, who was born in 1910. The youngest of the Hegyi children was born in 1914, a boy named István (He was the one who ended up in the death camp at Recsk).

My grandfather turned out to be a successful farmer and the land produced enough food and other goods for the family to have a comfortable life and even allow the children to have an education past the traditional fourth grade. Maria completed Grade 6 and Antal went beyond Grade School to graduate from a two-year forest technician course. After finishing Grade 6, my father was enrolled in a seminary to be trained for the priesthood (with strong persuasion from Grandmother). This lasted only two months. My father escaped the seminary through a second story window and went home to tell his father that he wanted to be a farmer just like him. Margit and Emi both finished Grade 6 and István was considered to be the brain, because he managed to graduate from Gimnázium, a four-year High School, after which he secured a well paying job in an office.

My grandfather had tears in his eyes each time he talked about the tragic day of June 1st, 1933 when my grandmother died of an illness which appeared to be a bad case of influenza. He never married again. Nobody could ever take the place of his true love. The oldest daughter, Maria, stepped in to run the house after the death of Grandmother, but she left the Hegyi home two years later to marry a *well to do* farmer in a neighboring village, Sótony.

My father had gradually taken over running of the farm and, as tradition would suggest, he started to look for a wife to help him with the chores. In 1935, he went to a dance in Püspökmolnári, a village about twenty kilometers from Nyögér, and met a petit young girl named Sarolta Piri. The girl was home for the weekend from the Eszterházi Castle near Sopron, where she worked as an assistant chef. After a two-year courtship, the thirty-three-year-old Ferenc married the twenty-four-year-old Sarolta. On June 9, 1938, I was born on the kitchen table, delivered by a midwife as was the custom in the village.

After hearing the story about our family's history, I realized that it was my turn as a second generation Hegyi (after grandfather) to follow the tradition of improving the life of the Hegyi family. Since I was not keen on working the land like my father, I started to see my destiny in office work. I had given up the idea of becoming a priest and even my mother had conceded to that fact, especially when she saw that I really liked girls. My grandfather's stories about the *big world* were also exercising my imagination about lands far away from our little village.

In June 1954, I finished first year of High School and in the summer I found a job in the office of the collective farms as a clerk. My job was to keep track of how much produce was brought into the storage, then monitor to where it was transported afterwards. My boss was the Secretary of the local Communist party. He was a very nice man and he treated me well. He was the first Communist that I actually liked.

My position in the office helped my father's treatment in the collective farm because his son was now working for the Secretary of the party. The villagers noticed that the Secretary treated me with respect and fairness. With the money I earned during the summer, I was able to buy clothes suitable to wear at High School. During the first year, I really looked the part of a peasant boy who came from a small village. But now, I looked like a small town High School student. My mother was very proud of me.

When Mother said to Father, "Look at your son. Doesn't he look handsome?" Father smiled approvingly.

However, he always replied, "I thought he looked pretty good in the young farmer's outfit, too when he was working with me."

Deep down in his heart, Father's dream was that I work the land with him. It was also a tradition in the village that the son or daughter who inherits the family home will look after the parents when they no longer could work.

During the second year of High School, I was getting good marks, writing poetry and I even started dating beautiful girls (writing love poems helped a lot). I was getting some recognition in reciting poetry with some passion, especially when some of those poems were my own. When my mother visited my High School during a parent-teacher meet session, one of my teachers told my mother that I was a good student, but a little bit too romantic.

In the summer of 1955, I resumed my job in the office of the collective farm. Antal Bácsi, the Secretary of the local Communist party was my boss again and he welcomed me back warmly. I enjoyed very much working for him. Because of his influence, I was actually starting to accept our lifestyle as it was developing.

The amnesty given to political prisoners by Prime Minister Imre Nagy released information to us about the cruelty of the Secret Police and Rákosi himself. The freed political prisoners, like my Uncle István, talked about their life under internment and the cruelty of the prison guards who wore AVH uniforms. In school, we were taught about the cruelty of the SS, but the AVH was just as bad, if not worse, in the treatment of innocent people who they accused of false charges.

I had difficulty in trusting the correctness of information that we were getting in school. Deep inside, I was rebelling against the cruelty of the Communist Regime. I was also influenced by my grandfather's comments that I represented the generation of Hegyi's who was expected to raise the family's standard of living.

Freedom Fighter

In 1955, a rapprochement between the Soviet Union and Yugoslavia produced the Belgrade Declaration, in which Moscow confirmed that each nation had the right to follow its own road to Socialism. One year later, Soviet leader, Nikita S. Khrushchev, denounced Stalin in his *Secret Speech* before the Twentieth Congress of the Soviet Communist Party on February 25, 1956. These external events shook Rakosi, who was a strong opponent of Titoism, a blind follower of Stalin and the instigator of Hungary's purges.

The Twentieth Congress of the Communist Party of Soviet Union (CPSU) marked a turning-point in the politics and ideology of the International Communist Movement. Although Khrushchev's secret speech revealing the crimes of Stalin was not to be published, news of it began to spread immediately after he read it out to trust Party leaders.

The Twentieth Congress placed insoluble tasks before the Hungarian Party leadership, which was still unchanged in composition. Rákosi was the one who had to head the de-Stalinization process in Hungary, unveil the mistakes and crimes of the past, and condemn the culprits, especially himself. Meanwhile, he had to make sure that the top Party leader (himself again) should not lose prestige.

Throughout the summer of 1956, the Soviets consistently insisted on integrating the most basic steps of de-Stalinization in Hungary. In other words, they insisted that the resolutions of the

Twentieth Congress be implemented. At the same time, the person responsible for the illegal acts committed had to be found, so as to vindicate the Soviets and the Socialist System. As early as 1953, there were efforts to shift the entire blame onto Gábor Péter, the former head of AVH, who was already in custody, but not executed like Beria his Soviet counterpart. When this did not succeed, attention focused on Mihály Farkas, Minister of Defense. He was a suitable scapegoat because he actually bore some responsibility. However, it soon emerged that Farkas was not a significant enough figure for the purpose. Even before the Twentieth Congress, the question of Rákosi's personal responsibility had been raised at a Party meeting.

There was mounting activity during this time of the Petőfi Circle which consisted of writers and other intellectuals. The Petőfi Circle began to give new direction and substance to the struggle against the Rákosi system. A succession of professional debates began to take place in May, where more and more sensitive issues were discussed before swelling audiences. It became possible for historians and philosophers, many of whom had been silenced before, to appear in public again. The National Association of People's Colleges was socially rehabilitated. At a debate in the Central Officers' Hall of the Hungarian People's Army on June 18, Júlia Rajk, widow of the executed Lászlo Rajk, publicly appealed for her husband's rehabilitation, while others pressed for the need to rehabilitate *a whole country, a whole people.*

Soviet Ambassador, Yury Anropov, included a description of the debate in his report to Moscow, saying he understood it had "essentially degenerated into a demonstration against the Party leadership." This was more than the authorities were prepared to tolerate, especially as the proposed discussion for the next meeting was the question of legality. The Central Committee of the HWP condemned and suspended the debates of the Petőfi Circle on June 30th.

Even under the iron fist of the Party, the Secret Police (AVH) was showing major upheavals. This was apparent in the rising number of voluntary resignations, even though the strength of the AVH was sharply reduced at the beginning of 1956. The conviction of its former leader, Gábor Péter, who previously had absolute authority, brought further dismissals and arrests.

The constant threat posed to AVH officers by the rehabilitations, with increasingly frequent calls being made for the culprits to be named and prosecuted, alarmed and weakened the service. Many of those released from prison were returning to the political leadership, where they could be expected to press for the prosecution of those who had imprisoned and tortured them. At one Political Committee meeting, János Kádár criticized the AVH personally. Even the chief Soviet adviser in Hungary for interior affairs reported back to Moscow that unhealthy feelings were spreading among some of the state security personnel as well.

In the summer of 1956, the Soviet leaders decided the time had come for a further political intervention in Hungary. The situation was causing concern not only for the Soviets, but throughout the Socialist camp where it was feared that 'unexpected, disagreeable events might occur.' The likelihood of this was increased by the demonstrations in Poland, where the security forces used arms to break up workers demonstrating for an improvement in living and working conditions. The clash cost almost a hundred lives and several hundred were wounded. To prevent any similar occurrence in Hungary, Anastas Mikoyan arrived in Budapest with a broad mandate to handle the crisis. Having gathered requisite information after his arrival, Mikoyan put forward two proposals for averting the crisis. Mikoyan acknowledged that Rákosi's dismissal was inevitable. Consequently, Rákosi was relieved of his main functions on July 21, 1956 on the grounds of ill health. He was exiled to the Soviet Union. The idea behind Rákosi's dismissal was to bring new blood into the party leadership. A new team, fully united in principle and practice, was created to address the most urgent tasks, such as dispersing the centres of opposition and completely ending the opposition agitation and propaganda.

However, Rákosi's replacement as First Secretary of the HWP was Gerö and he only made matters worse. Gerő's succession did nothing to win over those who were against Rákosi's policies. Division in the Party remained. Members were unable to reach a common position even on the most basic issues. Increasingly larger groups turned away from the leadership altogether.

For two straight months in 1956, writers and students challenged the Communist leadership. On October 22, 1956, the Technical University went even further. The meeting decided to formulate demands, influenced by the events in Poland. A demonstration of solidarity with the changes in Warsaw was announced for the next day. In a break from the usual formalities, what they addressed to the Party was not a petition, but a set of demands, reinforced by a street demonstration. Neither the press nor the radio would publish their demands in full and the students ruled out any compromise. Not to be thwarted in their bid for reconciliation, the students made stencilled copies instead, which they distributed on the streets, pasted on walls, and sent with delegations to the Budapest factories.[3] The students demanded a new Government constituted under the direction of Imre Nagy, and that all criminal leaders of the Stalin-Rákosi era must be immediately dismissed.

On October 23rd, students of the Budapest Technical University started a peaceful march to show their support for the Poles, to demonstrate that Hungary wanted to be politically and economically independent, and to end the Soviet occupation. They were joined by workers and others. Some went to the Bem statue; others went to the Petőfi statue, while another group went to tear down the Stalin statue because it represented Soviet dominance over Hungary.

Later that evening the students tried to broadcast their demands at the Hungarian Radio Station. The Radio Building was guarded by a detachment of the AVH. When the crowd began to threaten the building after a student

---

[3]*Crisis and a Search for Solutions.*

http://www.rev.hu/history_of_56/oral/index.htm

delegation was detained within, the AVH opened fire on the demonstrators which included women and children. This action killed several and wounded many more. This was the moment when the unrest and frustration of thousands of people turned from peaceful protest to revolution.

The news spread quickly. Disorder and violence erupted throughout the capital. The revolt spread across the country, several police stations and army units provided arms for the freedom fighters and the government fell. Thousands organized into militias, battling the State Security Police (AVH) and Soviet troops. Pro-Soviet Communists and AVH members were often hanged, shot or imprisoned, as former political prisoners were released and armed.

Local councils took over municipal control from the Communist Party and demanded political changes. Nagy formed a new government, abolished the AVH and said that negotiations had begun for the complete withdrawal of the Soviet troops. He also abolished the one-party system, declared its intention to withdraw from the Warsaw Pact and pledged to re-establish free elections. By the end of October, fighting had almost stopped and a sense of normality began to return[4].

---

[4] *1956 Hungarian Revolution.*

http://fog.ccsf.cc.ca.us/~sgati/gatiproductions/starting_over/revolution.htm.

Throughout all of this unrest in 1956, I was attending High School in Sárvár. I had just started my fourth year in the Gimnázium. On October 24th, I woke up at 6 a.m. at the place where my mother had arranged room and board for me during the school year. I turned on the radio and started to shave. At first, I thought that the reception was bad on the radio because I was hearing loud cracking noises.

I was startled when I heard the announcer say, in a highly excited voice, "Dear listeners, you are hearing the sound of machine guns. Yesterday, university students were peacefully demonstrating on the streets, and the AVH fired on them, killing many students, women and children and as a result, the fighting has now spread throughout Budapest. Hungary has erupted into a revolution."

I finished dressing and rode my bicycle to the High School at 8 a.m. There were many students outside the building. Everyone was talking about the revolution. One of our teachers came outside and told us to return home and wait until we were called back to school over the radio.

I rode my bicycle back to the place where I was living and told the land lady what was happening in Budapest. Mrs. Pasti was in her sixties, a widow without any children. She treated me like a grandson. We agreed that I might as well go home to my parents until this thing settled. I packed my books and clothes, strapped the suitcase on the back of the bicycle and started my ten kilometer trip to the village of Nyögér where my parents lived. I arrived home around noon. My parents were very excited that a revolution was in full swing in Budapest and that we might soon regain our freedom from the Soviet occupation.

I spent the afternoon visiting friends and speculating on what was going on in Budapest. We did not have television. Radio was the only medium to hear the news. Street names where the fighting was going on did not mean much to us. We noted one thing, though, that the students who were throwing Molotov cocktails on Russian tanks were about the same age or just a couple of years older than I was. My father commented that if I had been allowed to go to High School when I finished Grade 8, I would be at a University and very likely in the middle of the fighting.

In the evening at 6 p.m., there was a mass in our Roman Catholic parish church. The priest, Father Imre Lenarsics, was well known for his anti-Communist views. Not surprisingly, he delivered a compassionate message to the faithful to support the revolution. Our church was parish for two other villages, so there was only standing room as people were looking for some direction from the priest. Even during Communist control, everyone respected or feared the priest because he made it clear that we needed him to gives us absolution before we could go to heaven.

At the end of the mass, as people were coming out of church, Father Lenarsics was at the main door and suggested that somebody recite the patriotic poem of Petőfi which was an inspiration to the 1848 freedom fight against the Austrians. Since I was standing near the priest, several people volunteered me to do the honours. I was well known in the village for my theatrical

Journey to the Big World

activities, was a leading actor in a touring troupe, and often recited poetry on special occasions.

I did not have to be asked twice, Petőfi was my favourite poet and I knew the requested poem, *Talpra Magyar* (*Rise up Magyar*) by heart. I stood on the top of the stairs leading to the main entrance of the church, while the parishioners gathered around. I was about ten stairs above the ground so I could see the faces of the people waiting. I took my cap off, paused for a moment, and then started:

Rise up, Magyar, the country calls!	*Talpra magyar, hí a haza!*
It's 'now or never' what fate befalls...	*Itt az idő, most vagy soha!*
Shall we live as slaves or free men?	*Rabok legyünk vagy szabadok?*
That's the question - choose your `Amen'!	*Ez a kérdés, válasszatok!*
(Ref.)	*(Ref)*
God of Hungarians, we swear unto Thee,	*A magyarok Istenére Esküszünk,*
We swear unto Thee - that slaves we shall No longer be!	*Esküszünk, hogy rabok tovább Nem leszünk!*

I recited four verses and the crowd joined me with the refrain at the end of each verse. As I recited the refrain, I put my left hand on my heart and raised the right hand in a victory sign. The crowd followed me with this gesture and I could see elderly farmers with tears coming from their eyes. When I reached the end of the poem, the crowd gave me an enthusiastic applause like nothing I had ever experienced on stage.

My performance excited a lot of people and caused the establishment of a Revolutionary Youth Council. Since reciting the poem earned me some status in the village, I was nominated and acclaimed to be the Chairman of the Council. I accepted this honour and responsibility because I believed that Communism had to be defeated by the people who had been exploited by this cruel Regime.

When I went to bed that night, I couldn't sleep at all. So many thoughts were going on in my head. I was just elected as a student leader and we called ourselves *freedom fighters.* In Budapest, university students were risking their lives in the freedom fight. We heard on the radio that several army units had joined the revolution and were fighting the Soviet occupiers. One person came home from Budapest and told us that students were making Molotov cocktails and throwing them from the tops of buildings into open trucks carrying Russian soldiers.

I was faced with a difficult decision. Even though I recited the patriotic poem of Petőfi, I could still pull back and watch the events unfold. I could tell people in the morning that I didn't want to be Chairman of the Revolutionary Youth Council. *BUT*, then I reminded myself that each time I was shaving, I would look into the mirror and see a person who didn't have the guts to fight for what he believed and for his beloved country. My great-great grandfather had the guts to fight in the 1848 revolution for which he paid the ultimate price, his life. He brought honour to the Hegyi name and my grandfather installed in me the importance of fighting for what one's beliefs.

I knew what I had to do the next morning as I started to shave. I knew what I had to do in order to be proud of the face that I was shaving.

Our Youth Council met around 10 a.m. on October 25th. Angry villagers had already rounded up some of the local Communists and were ready to punish them. They were demanding to hang Eva the tax collector who was responsible for the heavy fines on people in order to force them into the collective farm. She was the one responsible for our family going without food during the winter of 1952. Farmers, including my father, were chanting hang the bitch. Antal Bácsi, the man who had given me a job in the summers, was also among the accused. Now I had the task of chairing his trial by the revolutionary tribunal. Many of the villagers were after blood. I felt that if we did that, we would be as bad as the AVH guards who tortured my Uncle István. I managed to convince the group that the real enemy was the Soviet occupiers. I suggested that we focus on helping the freedom fighters in Budapest and let the legal system deal with the local Communist leaders in due course. I was supported for this stand by the Youth Council and the Communist leaders were put under house arrest (the village had no jail).

I spent the next week organizing the shipment of food to Budapest to support the freedom fighters. Farmers were bringing flour, smoked meat, potatoes and canned fruit to the storage room of the collective farm. Antal Bácsi had the keys for the storage room. He came out to help us collect the food and even arranged with the driver of the truck owned by the collective farm to take the supplies to Budapest which was about a four-hour drive. Privately, he thanked me for my calmness during the trial. He was a man of high integrity, believed strongly in the principles of Communism, but he was not a supporter of the Stalin-Rákosi style of cruel Regime. Although he was Secretary of the local Communist party, he never hurt anyone even during the most repressive period of the Rákosi Regime.

There was jubilation in the village that Imre Nagy was negotiating the withdrawal of Soviet troops. Villagers were dancing in the streets when we heard that the government of Imre Nagy had also disbanded the AVH, promised free election, and gave notice to withdraw from the Warsaw pact.

The most important aspect of the political changes for the village people was the possibility of having enough food and money for clothing. While the cease of the AVL terror was welcome news, villagers gradually adjusted to the lifestyle that you couldn't trust your neighbours, friends or even your family members when it came to the AVH internment. Consequently, people just stopped talking about politics and the Regime. However, it was more difficult to accept the fact that the farmers worked hard every day while the Regime took away most of the produce, leaving insufficient amounts for the farmers to use.

People were very hopeful that Imre Nagy was on their side. He had a good knowledge of agriculture and a reputation of fairness towards the farmers. That was not to be. On November 4, 1956, the Red Army launched a major attack on Hungary aimed at crushing the spontaneous national uprising that had begun twelve days earlier.

At 5:20 a.m., Hungarian Prime Minister Imre Nagy announced the invasion to the nation in a grim, thirty-five-second broadcast, declaring, "Our troops are fighting. The Government is in its place." However, within hours Nagy himself would seek asylum at the Yugoslav Embassy in Budapest while his former colleague and imminent replacement, János Kádár, who had been flown secretly from Moscow to the city of Szolnok, sixty miles southeast of the capital, had taken over power with Moscow's backing.

As former Chairman of the Youth Revolutionary Council, I found myself facing the possibility of going to jail or even being shot. The news spread quickly that the police had started to round up students who were youth leaders in the revolution. Some of them were shot on the spot, while others were imprisoned. I went into hiding in the village, sleeping in barns and hay stacks, changing my location frequently.

On Sunday evening, November 18th, my grandfather brought me food to my hiding place and told me that he overheard in the smoke shop that a police captain, called Pallosi, who was originally from the village, but now was a senior police officer in a nearby town, was looking for me. He was telling people that he was looking for that Hegyi kid. He will be shot like the rest of the teenage terrorists.

For the last time, I sat on the knee of grandfather as I gave him a big hug, and then asked him what should I do? Should I come out of hiding or should I try to make it to Austria? Grandfather looked at me with tearful eyes and said, "Remember what they did to your Uncle István, I don't want that to happen to you, I love you grandson". We then stood and grandfather looked at me with a faraway look in his eyes and said: "Go to the *big world*, live our dream."

We both agreed that we shouldn't tell my parents about this plan because they would be too emotional to understand the danger that I was in. We then talked about how I could send a message back from Austria (if I made it) to let them know that I was safe without putting the family in harm's way. We agreed on a coded message through Radio Free Europe: "Golden lamb has arrived safely."

My grandfather said that he will be glued to the radio and when he hears this message, he will then talk to my parents. Knowing that this was the last time that I would see my grandfather was a deeply emotional moment for me. The tears blurred my vision as I watched his tall figure disappear into the darkness.

After I said goodbye to Grandfather, our Youth Revolutionary Council met for the last time. My cousin, Imre, who had returned home from Budapest, attended the meeting and told us that he was involved in throwing Molotov cocktails from the top of the buildings into armoured Soviet vehicles. He said that he

Journey to the Big World

was definitely going to try to escape to Austria because he would be executed for his activities during the revolution. He thought that our council members may not be in danger, but the youth leaders have already been declared terrorists and many of them had already been shot. This news, combined with the one Grandfather overheard in the smoke shop, left no doubt in my mind that, if I was captured, the probability of being shot the next day was very high.

Imre suggested that we try to escape together early the next morning while people in the village were still sleeping. I agreed and we started to develop a strategy for the escape. Two of our friends offered to take two bicycles out of the village at night and hide it at a location about one kilometer west of the village.

Early the next morning, while it was still dark, Imre and I, armed with only knives, started our escape journey. We agreed that we would not allow ourselves to be captured. If we were to run into the police or the Russians we would act cool. Should they try to capture us, the knives would come out and we would attack until they finished the job.

We managed to get out of the village without meeting anyone and to a nearby corn field which provided shelter from being seen. On the other side of the corn field, we found the two bicycles. We took the two bicycles with us and walked from one corn field to another, keeping our heads low, until we reached a dirt county road south of the village. That's where we felt safe enough to start riding the bicycles.

By noon, we arrived at the village of Püspökmolnári where my maternal grandfather, Piri, lived. I explained to my grandfather the danger we were in and asked for help. He tried to talk us out of leaving Hungary, but when I told him that a high ranking police officer was looking for me and was planning to shoot me, he agreed that we should leave Hungary. Grandfather Piri then gave us food and direction on how to get to Austria. The village was not too far from the border, although it was no longer safe to travel on the main roads because they were heavily patrolled by both the Hungarian police and Russian soldiers.

We left the bicycles with Grandfather Piri and started our journey on foot, avoiding the main roads. We walked in a westerly direction, hiding in corn fields and small woodlots, but keeping sight of the main road to Graz. We could see that the main road to Austria was heavily patrolled by soldiers traveling in large trucks. At one point, as we were walking in a woodlot which was at the edge of the highway, we could see a lorry full of Hungarian policemen. We hid behind some bushes until they drove off then ran out to cross the highway to get into a village on the other side.

An elderly farmer saw us and waved to us to go over to him. We ran fast to meet him and he said that we must hide in a haystack because the policemen knew that we were in the woodlot. They had left in an attempt to draw us out, but they were expected back right away. We eased ourselves into the side of the haystack about two feet deep and lay there motionless. True enough, the police came back. They questioned the farmer who said that he did not see anyone. Then, the police started to search his stables, barn and the yard. One policeman came over to the haystack and started to shove his bayonet into the area where we lay. I felt one stab on my left side, the next one on my right side; both missed me by about a foot. It was tough to lie there without panicking, but we survived and the police went away. When all was clear, the farmer came back and said that we could come out.

We asked the farmer to help us by showing the way to the border. He asked, "How much money you have?" We did not have much, so he settled for valuables. I had a raincoat which was almost new. I gave it to him even though it was getting cold. I also gave him a pocket watch which was my treasured possession from Grandfather. My cousin also gave him his overcoat and some other valuables. The farmer walked with us for twenty minutes and showed us the direction to the border. He said that we would have to cross the highway again because that was the shortest way to get to Austria.

We then parted company and Imre and I started the last leg of our journey. As we were getting closer to the highway, which had a lot of traffic, we were crawling to avoid detection. When the coast appeared to be clear, we stood up and started to walk towards the highway, trying to cross it. Suddenly, an armoured car full of Russian soldiers appeared. We thought that was the end for us.

In a moment of total defiance, I said to Imre, "Act cool. I will talk to them."

The Russian soldiers stopped and surrounded us, machine guns pointed at our heads. I still don't know where I got the strength and the wisdom to act this scene out. Having studied Russian for six years, I greeted them in their language, saying, "Hello comrades. We are pleased to see the Red Army coming to help us. We are young Communists (Komsomol), High school Students, just going home. Our village is near the border." I showed them my membership card in the Young Communist Organization (all High School students were automatically enrolled).

The soldiers greeted us warmly. They were just a few years older than we were, and were happy that I communicated with them in their own language. The soldiers offered us cigarettes and waved to us goodbye as they pooled away in the armoured car. I thanked them for their kindness and for coming to help Hungarians. We quickly crossed the highway and disappeared into another woodlot. Now, we were close to the border.

In the woodlot, we met many other refugees. We stopped to strategize on how to cross the border. We were standing on the side of a strip of land freshly ploughed when someone suggested that it could be mined. At that point, I just wanted to get it over with. I knew that I did not want to go to prison; there was no return to my parent's house; and living did not appear to be a desirable option. I volunteered to crawl across the border strip to see if it was mined. At that point in time, I had had enough and the possibility of being blown up did not frighten me at all.

Everyone stood in silence as I started my journey, lying on my stomach, pooling myself one elbow after another. At each move, I expected to be blown up. It was the longest ten minutes of my life before reaching Austria. When I reached the other side, I stood up beside a tree and watched as about 200 refugees crawled on my track, one after another. Everyone made it safely and the ordeal was over. With tearful eyes, I said goodbye to my beloved motherland.

Re-Building a Shattered Life

After crossing the border, the Austrian police escorted us to a school where all refugees were registered. While waiting to be interviewed, I was reflecting on what had happened. I was eighteen years old, did not speak German or English, just lost my country and parents and the future which appeared to be so bright just a few month ago was now so full of uncertainties. I sent a message home to my Grandfather through Radio Free Europe "the golden lamb arrived safely".

We stayed in a refugee camp near Graz, Austria for about ten days. We were told that we could not stay in Austria much longer. The Red Cross brought in delegations who talked about what they offered for the refugees in their country. United States, Canada and Australia were popular choices by the older refugees, especially couples with children. Singles and students were generally given rather limited choices. When the delegation from England asked who was interested in going to London, Imre and I stood up quickly and were lucky enough to be selected for an interview by English Immigration Officers with the help of Hungarian-English interpreters.

We went through a series of interviews, questioned at length about why we left Hungary and what were our views about Britain and the political system there. I was honest and told them that I knew very little about Britain, except what the Communists were telling us which were different from what we learned from listening to Radio Free Europe. As a student, I read some of

Journey to the Big World

Shakespeare's works in Hungarian and that was the extent of my knowledge.

After the interviews, we waited for about twenty-four hours before being called back by an English Immigration Officer who gave us the good news that we were being offered political refugee status by the British Government. The next day, those of us who were scheduled to go to Britain were transported by buses to the railway station in Graz. We were escorted into the passenger cars by the police who locked all of the doors firmly once we were inside. The long journey then began through the snow covered mountains to Salzburg where a British Airways plane was waiting for us.

There was no food on the train so we were getting very hungry long before reaching Salzburg. Fortunately, the train stopped a few times in small villages and people were giving us some bread, cheese and water through the windows. When we reached the Salzburg airport, we were taken into a large hangar where two rows of tables had lots of bread, cheese and juice. We weren't sure when we would receive food again, so I pigged out on cheese. We boarded the airplane and I experienced my first airplane flight. We hadn't even left Austrian air space when I realized that I had made a mistake eating all of that cheese before the flight. For at least ten years after that experience, I could not even look at cheese, let alone eat it.

Journey to the Big World

Picture 4. Me as a refugee.

When we arrived in London, we were taken to the army barracks in Aldershot. The Red Cross gave us some secondhand clothes, and then we were allowed to wander around the base and talk to other refugees from Hungary. Since the gates were guarded by British soldiers, we did not see much of England. We went through more interviews to try to get relocated somewhere in Britain. Refugees who had a trade were the first ones to get placed. I was just an eighteen-year-old High School dropout. Not exactly a much sought after commodity.

We spent about a week wondering when we would be allowed to leave the army barracks and meet some English people. Then one morning, Imre and I were called in to the Red Cross office and were told that we had been selected to go to Halifax, Yorkshire, where the Salvation Army was offering accommodation for ten Hungarian refugees until we could find a job. We traveled to Halifax by bus. It was the first time we had a chance to look at the English countryside, which was so different from the land we had left behind. We came from a part of Hungary that had fields of agricultural crops, previously divided into small parcels, but after the collectivization the countryside had been transformed into large fields of wheat, rye, barley, corn and potatoes. What was in front of us consisted of small 'tablets' of grasslands separated by stone walls and scattered woodlots.

We arrived in Halifax late in the evening and couldn't figure out why people standing outside the bus had yellow faces. That's when we noticed that the street lights which had yellow bulbs so they could function better when the fog descended on the city. As we got off the bus, we were met by a nice English lady, Mrs. Dillinger, who spoke good Hungarian. She told us that we can stay in the hostel until we get a job and that she will help us to integrate into the English society. The captain, who was in charge of the hostel seemed very kind, shook hands with each of us and said through Mrs. Dillinger: "Welcome to Halifax, I hope you will enjoy your stay with us".

My first night in the Salvation Army hostel was a bad experience. Many of the local guests were heavily intoxicated and were walking around in an apparent daze. I made a mistake of choosing the lower bunk bed without checking out who was in the upper bunk. Well, the guy who occupied the upper bunk was drunk and wet the bed and some drops were coming down to where I was lying. I went to the bathroom to clean up and when I came back I found that someone stole from my jacket the 10 shillings that the Red Cross gave me. At that time I had no idea of the value of 10 shillings, I didn't think it would buy a lot of things, but I was looking forward to going out of the hostel the next day to look around and buy some bread and salami (the type of food that I was used to in Hungary).

I sat up all night on the side of the bed and went through a wide range of emotions. It was December and near Christmas. I thought of my parents wondering where I was. Perhaps it would have been better if I hit a land mine when I was crawling across the border. Why did I have to recite that poem anyway? If I hadn't, I would be back in High School and preparing for Law School. Now, here I was among the drunks, with no money, no job, and no one to turn to. My desperation quickly turned into anger and I told myself that nobody would ever piss on me again!

In the morning, I told Mrs. Dillinger what had happened. She arranged that I had the ten shillings replaced by the hostel. Imre and I then went out on our own and experienced for the first time how to cope when you can't speak a word of the local language. We went into a Café and asked for coffee and showed our money so that the waitress would take what it cost.

Since the coffee cost less than one shilling, we experimented by buying some food. Of course, we didn't know the name of any of the foods. We had no dictionary, so we pointed to one of the meals that somebody was having at the next table, which looked like a bun with meat in it. All we knew in English was *okay*, so we just pointed to the bun and said *okay*? The nice lady who was the waitress was very friendly, talked to us in English, but we had no idea what she was saying. We just sat there and drank the coffee. About ten minutes later, she returned to our table with two buns filled with meat and placed them in front of us. We showed her our money again. She just smiled and took from each of us three shillings and giving us 6 pence back.

This was our first lesson in purchasing food. We learned later from Mrs. Dillinger in the hostel that the food we ate was called a hamburger and that it cost two shillings and six pence. At that point, I questioned Mrs. Dillinger if she was sure that the food was hamburger because it had beef in it and not ham. She had a good laugh over that one and said that there were a lot of unique expressions in the English language that we would need to get used to.

Just before Christmas, I was invited up to the suite of the Salvation Army Captain who was in charge of the hostel. He was very sympathetic to my situation as he explained through Mrs. Dillinger. He gave me an English Hungarian Dictionary which had only 500 words. That was my introduction to learning English. I treasured that Dictionary and kept it for years.

Two days before Christmas, Mrs. Dillinger, invited six of us refugees to live with her in a rented cottage near Hebden Bridge. While I was very grateful for the Salvation Army for looking after us when we had arrived in Halifax, I was happy for the change of scenery that was offered by Mrs. Dillinger. In the cottage, she told us a little bit about herself. She told us that she had married a Hungarian journalist and lived in Budapest for years. When the revolution broke out, she left for Austria with her ten-year-old son, but her husband stayed behind. She still didn't know what had happened to him. We were very lucky that she decided to take us in and look after us.

Journey to the Big World

I remember Christmas Eve, 1956. I felt extremely sad and alone. My thoughts were with my parents and the home I had left behind. I remembered the previous Christmas as we decorated the tree, my sister and I were hanging the decorations and the homemade candy wrapped in fancy paper. We drank hot chocolate and were singing Christmas carols. Now, I was alone, very much alone. I went outside and sat on the stone fence and cried my heart out. Why this had to happen to me? What am I going to do from now on? I didn't speak a word of English, I had no family and I had never lived on my own before. My parents had always been there to look after me. It was the saddest Christmas that I ever spent. At the same time, it was the beginning of the process of rebuilding a shattered life.

In early January, with the help of Mrs. Dillinger, Imre and I secured a job in Hebden Bridge at Austin Brothers Textile Factory, pressing trousers. I still remember the joy I felt when I was handed my first pay cheque: nine pounds for a week's work. I was able to give some to Mrs. Dillinger for the room and board and had enough to buy a raincoat.

I was learning English from the Dictionary and mastered such expressions as "Yes...No... Thank you... Good morning." I had come from a very religious background where the reply to "Good morning" was always, "May God give (or God Bless)." Of course I could not find this expression in my little dictionary, so I decided to experiment. When I went to work next morning, I turned to my co-worker called Gilbert on my right and said, "Good morning."

He replied, "Good morning."

Journey to the Big World

I was confused because I was expecting to hear different words and not a repeat of the same greeting. I tried to rationalize why this happened and at that point I remembered that my father used to say that the English people were very polite. I concluded that Gilbert must have tried to greet me at the same time and the two "Good mornings" were coincidences.

I was determined to complete my experiment and an hour later, turned to Gilbert again and said, "Good morning."

He looked at me kind of funny and said, "Good morning."

Well, when you don't speak the language, the brain does not seem to work at full potential. It never occurred to me that I just heard the proper response. Determined as I was to get a different answer, I waited another half an hour and said to him again, "Good morning."

At that point he turned to me sort of friendly, and replied with a different expression, which included a hand gesture of lifting two fingers (the middle one in both hands) towards me. I was too busy trying to remember the words. I decided that I could learn the hand gesture later. I wrote down in Hungarian phonetics the response my co-worker told me and started to memorize it.

At around 11 a.m., Mr. Austin (the senior partner of Austin Brothers) came on the floor to find out how we Hungarian refugees were doing. He came to me, shook my hands in a friendly manner and said, "Good morning".

I thought this was a good opportunity for me to show off my new knowledge of the language and responded with pride. In a very polite manner, broad smile and while clicking my heels, I told Mr. Austin, "F...off."

He smiled at I took my dictionary and we together worked out his question, "Who taught you that?" In the background, the other workers were having a good laugh. Gilbert conveniently went for a long session in the washrooms. I was quickly understanding that my response probably did not mean, "May God give," or "God Bless." According to Imre, who informed me later, I turned very red in the face when I realized that what I had said was very rude.

Picture 5. Mrs. Dillinger sitting on my knee.

Imre and I gradually drifted apart. He liked to drink in pubs and then take home one of the local girls for the night *to roll in bead* as he used to call it. When I told him that I wanted to continue my High School education, he told me that I was crazy to wish for impossible things because they would never happen. He also didn't like pressing trousers. Through some Hungarian refugee connections, he secured a better paying job in Leeds, Yorkshire, and moved there to live. I remember visiting him one weekend. I went on a double-decker bus on a Saturday morning and when I arrived in Leeds, I needed direction to the address where Imre was living. I practiced with Mrs. Dillinger how to ask for directions and managed to say in perfect English, "Excuse me please. I do not speak any English. Could you help me" As I approached people, they just turned away and shook their heads. I then realized that my sentence was too polished, so I changed to my own grammar and said, "Excuse me. No speak English. Help find address." After that people were wonderful. One lady even walked with me for two blocks and showed me the door where Imre lived.

Imre had become friends with some Hungarians who were heavy drinkers. I went with them on Saturday night to the pub. The next morning, I discovered that five to six pints of bitter in one night was directly related to an Excedrin headache. On Sunday morning, I went back to Halifax on the bus with a king-sized hangover. I decided that I would never again spend much time in the pubs.

In March 1957, I was offered lodgings by a group of middle-aged Hungarian miners who were making good money and were sharing the rent of a house. I could live there without paying for rent or food as long as I cleaned the house and cooked for them. I accepted the offer eagerly. I knew how to clean, but cooking was new to me. They were kind enough to teach me, although at times when the meal was not to their liking, they would throw it on the floor, and then I had to clean it up while they went out to eat in a restaurant. It was a very effective way of teaching me how to cook. After all, I was only eighteen years old. I was determined to master the art of cooking even though at that time I had to start with learning how to boil water.

Since I was learning English faster than the miners, they asked for my help in buying condoms. I used my Salvation Army dictionary to make the translation. We went to Boots to buy this commodity. They gave me money and I went inside, feeling very shy and nervous. I waited until the Pharmacist (a man) was alone and asked him for a box of rubbers. He said, "Okay." I bought the package, went outside and gave it to the miners. They opened it and it was a box of rubber bands. We all wondered how the English were practicing birth control. One of the guys even commented, "This must be painful."

The miners were Roman Catholics and they took me to church one Sunday morning. We met the priest who was friendly, although I couldn't help but wonder why he did not offer his help when we really needed it. Now that we had a little bit of money to put in the collection plate, he was eager to welcome us as Roman Catholics. After mass, we were invited to a reception in the church hall and some of the parishioners received us warmly. I was lucky to have been approached by a very nice couple, Mr. and Mrs. Gillespie. Of course, the conversations were rather

Journey to the Big World

limited, as my English was still within the scope of about 500 words.

As we said goodbye, Mrs. Gillespie said that I was invited to their place for lunch next Sunday after mass. I was extremely pleased by the invitation. I even bought a new suit for the occasion. During the week prior to that Sunday, I came down with a bad cold. People in the factory were very friendly to me and asked how I was. I would reply with the only expression that I knew, "Very well, thank you."

One of my co-workers laughed at me that I was giving the wrong answer and tried to correct it. He told me to say, in a Yorkshire accent, "I am not well. I have a bloody awful cold."

Next Sunday at lunch, Mrs. Gillespie asked me how I was. Well, I replied with the new expression. She smiled at me warmly and corrected my English. After that, she decided to be my benefactor and English teacher. I was a regular guest at their place on Sundays after mass. They had two beautiful daughters, Maureen and Katherine, who were just a few years older than I. I was accepted by them as their little brother. They even fixed me up with dates.

Life was good. I had a job and a wonderful family who looked out for me. I was learning English and started to think about my future. I told Mrs. Gillespie that I wanted to finish my High School education. She asked Mr. Gillespie to arrange a meeting with the Principal of the night school in Halifax. Mr. Gillespie was very influential around town. He was Managing Director of a Mackintosh Toffee Factory.

Mrs. Gillespie took me to meet the Principal of the High School, who agreed to take me in, provided that I passed an entrance exam. They thought it would be fair if the exam was in mathematics, given the fact that my English was still limited. I was very nervous as I went to take the written exam. The Principal was a very kind man and offered me different sets of problems that I was to solve. In Hungary I had been studying Calculus, so I went for that set of questions.

A few days after the exam, Mrs. Gillespie met me and said that the Principal was impressed with my exam results. I had passed a set of exams which were at the level of first-year University. I was ecstatic that I could go to night school to finish that part of my education. This was in June and the night school would start in September. Unknown to me, Mrs. Gillespie used her many contacts and, at a luncheon after mass, she told me the most incredible news. She had arranged for me to be accepted at the University of Edinburgh as a foreign student, with a World University Services scholarship which paid the fees to the University and gave me nine pounds per week. This was about the same as I was making in the factory.

Picture 6. Mrs. Gillespie and her family at Maureen's wedding.

Well, I didn't think that it would be wise for me to study law in English. In Hungary, I had worked on a farm and in the woods, so I thought that I would like to study forest engineering. Within a month, I received a letter from Dr. Charles Taylor, Director of Studies, at the Faculty of Forestry, University of Edinburgh, informing me that I had been accepted to study forest engineering, provided that I passed an English exam for foreign students. I was very happy for this opportunity and so was Mrs. Gillespie. I thanked her for getting me ready for the future.

On September 2nd, I took the train to Edinburgh. Mrs. Gillespie had made reservation for me at a student hostel called Manor Club, a hostel for foreign students, run by Mr. and Mrs.

McDonald. I shared a room with Yatendra Dixit from New Delhi, India. Yatendra and I became best friends and spent a lot of time together during that first year. From Yatendra, I learned a lot about the Indian culture, music and the wonderful curries.

Picture 7. My roommate at Edinburgh, Yatendra Dixit

During this time, Mr. Nehru, Prime Minister of India, visited Edinburgh. I found out that my friend, Yatendra, came from the prominent Dixit family. He was invited to meet Mr. Nehru in a private audience. I was fortunate to go with him and shake hands with Mr. Nehru. For a boy from a small village in Hungary, it was an experience of a lifetime to meet the *Dove of Peace*, as he was called at that time. I wrote to my grandfather about this important event. My mother replied that Grandfather was so happy that he broke into tears. That was the last communication that I had from Grandfather. He died a few days after he read my letter.

The day Grandfather died, which was unknown to me at the time, I felt his presence around me. He was with me at night, telling me to keep on fighting. This gave me extra strength for facing the challenges of passing exams in a language that I hadn't mastered yet.

University years were challenging. Dr. Taylor informed me that in order to keep my scholarship, I had to pass, in two weeks, the final exam in English for foreign students. In addition, I had to score at least 33% during the term exams, in Chemistry I (general science), Botany I (general science), Zoology I (general science) and Physics I (applied science). The Hungarian students who were taking the same exam that I had to in English had already taken English classes for eight months. There were only two classes left before the final exam. I attended those two classes and found that I understood more than the other students, mainly because I had to survive in English in an environment where Hungarian was rarely spoken. The other students, on the other hand, lived in a hostel where they all spoke Hungarian except when they were in class. The professor, who was originally from Hungary, gave us a list of essays that the final exam would be based on.

I reviewed the list and chose to read in detail George Orwell's, shooting *an Elephant*. I was interested in the story Orwell presented in the essay, it had similar messages that my grandfather had taught me. I particularly liked the sentence: "when the white man turns tyrant it is his own freedom that he destroys",[5] an expression that became a guiding light for me. I lucked out because the exam included a translation of a passage from this essay from English to Hungarian. I could even translate the expression "garish clothes" and as a result I received the highest mark in the class. This made me rather unpopular with the other Hungarian students. Deep down, however, I was convinced that Grandfather's spirit was looking out for me.

During the first term, I wrote my lecture notes half in English and half in Hungarian. Then, in the evenings, I would translate my notes, using a dictionary so that I could fully understand what the professor was saying. I managed quite well in classes where I only needed to listen, but the tutorials were particularly difficult where I had to interact with other students and the teachers. I was very nervous when someone asked me a question. I worried that my answer might be off the topic due to not understanding the questions.

One of the most embarrassing moments came during a Chemistry tutorial. I was near the end of a two-hour experiment. All I had to do was finish the titration. One of the professors, who was always very serious, came up behind me and stared at my work. I was so nervous that I knocked down the experiment. He

---

[5] George Orwell. *Essays and Articles*. 1936. *Shooting an Elephant*.

just looked at it and said loudly so that all of the hundred students in lab could hear, "Hegyi, do you always work in a pig sty?"

I replied, "Not until you came Sir."

This made everyone laugh, except the professor who walked away pretty mad. I didn't understand what had happened. I thought that I was telling him that my bench was clean until he made me nervous because he was watching me. After the class, one of the other students explained to me how my reply to the professor had been interpreted.

Another embarrassing incident occurred at a Marks and Spencer store just before Christmas in 1957. I had saved enough money to send a present to my parents. I saw a nice negligee in the window. I thought my mother would like that and even my father would appreciate it. In addition, it wouldn't cost too much to send it by air mail to Hungary. I went into the store to the ladies department and located the area where the negligees were displayed on hangers. Not knowing what size my mother would wear, I decided to get help. I looked around and located a lady who was about the same size as my mother. Not being quite fluent in English to explain what I needed, I asked her with a thick accent, "What size of negligee do you wear?"

She looked at me kind of funny and asked, "What are you a pervert?"

Not knowing the meaning of the word pervert, I just nodded my head and smiled. At that point she waved over some people in uniform who escorted me to the back office and they started to question me. When I managed to explain what I wanted, the security officers called in the sales lady and explained my predicament. After she had a good chuckle, she was very helpful, even wrapped the present for me. She said that she had a son about my age and if he was in a foreign country and would send her a nice negligee like that, she would be very proud. When I returned to the hostel, I looked up the word pervert and consequently went about ten shades of red.

The university was very kind to me. During the first year, I was allowed to take an English-Hungarian dictionary into each exam. I handed in the dictionary to the exam supervisor the day before so that they could examine it to ensure that there were no cheat notes in it. When I arrived to take the exam, they would hand me the dictionary so that I could translate the questions. Once I finished translating the questions, I gave the dictionary back to the supervisor, then proceeded to write the responses to the questions.

At the end of each term, I managed to get over 33% in all four science subjects, so my scholarship was secure. At the end of the first year, I passed Botany and Zoology, but I had to repeat the year for Chemistry and Physics. The repeat year was much easier, my English was rapidly improving, and I was able to understand the professors. I no longer needed to take the dictionary with me to translate the exam questions. As a result, I had time for social activities and started to go out with other students, especially with young ladies from America and Sweden. During the summer of 1958, I started dating an American exchange student, Judy Moran. She was a second year student from New York City who came to Edinburgh to study European history. I learned a lot from Judy about America and promised myself that one day I would definitely visit both the United States and Canada.

In January 1959, I moved out of the Manor Club to a flat near Hay Market. I rented this flat with three other students: Helmut from Germany, Eduardo from Spain, and Kenny from Burma. Miss Boyd was our landlady. She was about fifty years old, had never married and, according to Eduardo, she preferred women to men. On weekends, she would have her lady friend stay overnight. I used to serve them coffee in bed.

Eduardo was the oldest and most knowledgeable among us. He smoked a pipe, which made him look sophisticated. He never had any problem attracting beautiful girls to date him. He finished his law degree in Spain and came to Edinburgh to take some courses in English. Helmut was a third year Political Science student who came to Edinburgh to take some International Business classes. Kenny was a Burmese prince who was taking first year Biochemistry. We took turns cooking, but gradually I was elected to do the main meals. Helmut would wash the dishes, Eduardo would dry them and we trusted Kenny only with putting the dishes away. Kenny had servants at home and was used to being served. He tried to continue that lifestyle with us, but we worked on him right away, helping him to integrate into Western Society.

Kenny tried to sleep in the morning while we were preparing breakfast, expecting to be awakened only when breakfast was ready. One Saturday morning, we rolled the bed out of the bedroom into the hall while Kenny was still sleeping in it. I asked Miss Boyd to help us wake him up. She came out of her bedroom with a big smile and said, "Wake up Kenny," pulling off his blanket. She let out a loud scream and ran back to her bedroom. Kenny was lying there naked and was obviously dreaming about beautiful girls! Kenny then woke up in a hurry, ran into our bedroom, dressed and joined us while we were still laughing at the situation. After that, Kenny was the first one to get out of bed, especially on the weekends.

Picture 8. My twenty-first birthday party.

In February 1959, I met a nice Scottish girl, Elizabeth Murray. She was in the final year of a B.A. program majoring in English. Elizabeth helped me a lot with my English, as well as introduced me to an artistic life style that included going to concerts and visiting historical places. We attended a concert in the Usher Hall where Yehudi Menuhin, the famous violinist, was the virtuoso. In Hungary, I had only heard gypsies playing the violin in a manner that the instrument was *talking* to you. I was absolutely fascinated with the skills Mr. Menuhin was exhibiting during the concert. Elizabeth was delighted. Another memorable occasion was when Elizabeth and I went to a Student Union jazz festival where the Rector of the University, Sir James Robertson Justice, was the Master of Ceremonies.

I successfully passed the final exams in Chemistry and Physics in June 1959 and my forestry education started in a few months later. I found the forestry courses much easier and was getting generally good marks, while still having enough time for social activities. Elizabeth moved to Glasgow after graduating in June 1959. I visited her there a few times, but the relationship was gradually fading away. I was focusing on my studies and went out only a few times, but rarely on a date. Since the Forestry Faculty was close to the Student Nurses Residence, any time we needed dates to go for a dance in the Students Union Hall, we had no problem in getting student nurses to go with us. I also joined the International House on Princess Street where foreign students used to get together for a coffee or a beer to give moral support for each other. In October, I went for a Saturday night dance in the International House and my Egyptian friends had a nice looking Scottish girl in their group. Her name was Audrey Sutherland. I asked Audrey for a dance and we were having so much fun dancing and talking that we forgot to go back to the table until after they played the last dance.

Audrey told me that I was a good dancer. She especially liked my jokes, which was good because I had a never ending supply of them. After the dance, I accompanied Audrey to her home. We caught a bus on Princess Street. It took twenty minutes to reach the last stop in the suburb. We disembarked and walked the ten minutes that it took to the house where she lived with her parents. Before saying goodbye, we made a date for the next day. I walked back to the bus station, just to find that I had missed the last bus. I managed to get back to the flat by hitchhiking. It was after 3 o'clock in the morning when I finally climbed into to bed.

I couldn't sleep the rest of the night. I remembered what Grandfather told me about his first dance with Grandmother. Even my father had met my mother at a dance. Audrey and I started going steady and continued to have a good time. On Saturday, October 31, 1959, she invited me to meet her parents. I was nervous and was determined to impress her parents. I bought a bouquet of flowers for Mrs. Sutherland and when Audrey introduced me to her parents, I handed over the flowers by saying, "Mrs. Sutherland, here is a bucket of flowers for you."

Audrey corrected my pronunciation of the word *bouquet* and everyone had a polite chuckle over my English. Next I wanted to impress Mr. Sutherland by telling him one of the Scottish jokes that I had shared with Audrey the first night while we were dancing.

"Mr. Sutherland," I said, "have you heard about the two Scots men who bet each other a penny who could stay under the water longest and they both drowned?"

This one didn't go down well and Audrey explained later that when she told me that her Dad would really like this one, she didn't mean it the way I understood it. In any case, I was accepted into the Sutherland family. I came to know her two brothers, Ian and Gordon. Ian was the oldest, and a really friendly person. He and I got along well. Gordon was Audrey's younger brother. He never accepted me into the family. As a result, we had a polite, but distant relationship.

In November 1959, a very strange thing happened. Audrey's girlfriend Val was visiting from Aberdeen. The two of them decided to go to a fortuneteller. The fortuneteller was an old Gypsy lady. She read Audrey's fortune and told her that, although she had been planning to go to America, she had met a man with an accent whom she was going to marry. Also, she told Audrey to make the most of life because she wouldn't live past thirty-two years. This really frightened Audrey, especially when I asked her to marry me. She admitted that she was about to book her passage to America when she had met me, but she delayed it because she wanted to see how our relationship would develop. In any case, she accepted my proposal even though I had one more year left before graduating. She continued to be concerned about the second half of the fortuneteller's prediction.

Mr. and Mrs. Sutherland were delighted with the news that we were going to get married, although they were a bit surprised when we told them that we planned to do it right away. We reassured them that Audrey was not expecting. It was just that we were in love and we wanted to spend all of our time together. Besides, Audrey told them that two can live cheaper than one.

Initially, we planned to marry in a Roman Catholic Church even though Audrey's parents were very active in the Presbyterian Church. When the priest told Audrey that her parents would have to convert as well to the only church that offered salvation, we both decided to marry in a Presbyterian church where Mr. Sutherland was an elder.

The wedding was on February 20, 1960 and was presided over by Rev. Findlay. His wife, Muriel, was in charge of all the arrangements, including music. Audrey's favorite hymn was the *The Lord is My Shepherd.* It was played as she walked up to the altar with her father. After the ceremony, my forestry classmates formed an arch with axes as we walked out of the church. The reception was in a hotel where we started with a series of toasts, drank wine and danced to a live band. I found it particularly moving when Audrey and I danced to the first number played by the band, *Oh how we danced on the night we were wed*, which was my favorite. It was a song made popular by Al Jolson.

After the reception, we changed in one of the rooms and were taken by taxi to the railway station, heading to Aberdeen for the honeymoon. Audrey's grandmother had a flat in Aberdeen. While the grandmother was with Audrey's Mom in Edinburgh, we stayed in her flat for free. This suited us fine because we didn't have much money and staying in a hotel was a little bit rich for us.

After we let ourselves in, the most obvious next move was to go to bed. When I sat down on the bed to take my socks off, I heard the doorbell go off. I went to open the door, but no one was there. I came back to the bedroom and as Audrey sat down on the bed, the doorbell rang again. We then realized that the bed was wired, each time you pushed it down, the doorbell would ring. We called back to Edinburgh and Granny was having a good laugh as she told everyone that she had hired an electrician to do the wiring. She was very proud of herself and pleased that it worked. We didn't know how to unhook the device so we ended up putting the mattress on the floor to bypass the door connection.

Picture 9. My graduation from University of Edinburgh

Audrey and I moved into a small flat which had a sitting room, bedroom, bathroom and a kitchenette. She worked as a lab technician and earned about the same amount of money as my scholarship. The two of us were able to live cheaper than when we were both single. During the summer and over the

Christmas holiday, I worked in the McEwan's Brewery on Fourth Bridge, and made some extra money to help with the budget in buying clothes and taking my wife out to dances. Working in the brewery was quite an experience. That was the first time I came into contact with the Trade Union Movement in Britain. Under Communism, trade unions had no say in the working conditions and rates of pay. Their sole purpose was to arrange holidays and vacation trips for the workers. Since the Government claimed to represent the working people and proletariat, the Communists claimed that there was no need for any other organization to represent the working class. We were often told by the Communist leaders: "Comrades, you don't need to think, the state thinks for you." The Communist propaganda also told us how suppressed the Trade Union Movement was in the west.

When the foreman, Mr. Hamilton, pulled me aside and said, "Son, you are new to this country so I thought I should explain a couple of things to you. Work at the same speed as your co-workers."

I answered, "Okay." I really didn't understand why he had to tell me that.

Tommy, one of my co-workers saw the confused look on my face. He confided in me that the shop steward had complained to Mr. Hamilton that I was working too hard and making the other laborers look bad. Tommy said, "Just relax and work like we do."

After that, I made sure that I fitted in with the labor practices and had a chuckle about the Communist propaganda claiming that the labor unions were suppressed in the west.

As a married student, my focus increased on passing exams and my marks improved. In June 1961, I graduated with a B.Sc. degree in Forest Engineering.

After graduation from college, the next challenge was to get a job. My first option was to get into forestry in Britain. The British Forestry Commission had only a few openings in 1961 and, as a foreigner, I did not want to compete with British graduates. I decided to apply for a job overseas under the British system, which was the Colonial Office. In July 1961, I received a letter from the Colonial Office to go for an interview in London. The job was Assistant Conservator of Forests in Northern Rhodesia. I was excited about the opportunity, especially because we were expecting our first child in November.

I bought a new suit, had my hair cut and took the train to London. The interview was at 2 p.m. The train arrived around noon, so I had time to eat some lunch. The interview was near Piccadilly Circle, and as I was going into the building, a nasty pigeon dumped on my head. Of course, I could not go to the interview with that substance on my head, so I ran to the nearest washroom to clean myself. After I made myself presentable, I ran up to the interview room, ten minutes late.

The first question the Chairman asked me was, "Mr. Hegyi, why are you late?"

Was I to tell him the truth? Suffice it to say that I just apologized without giving the reason. Then the interview started. It was obvious that I did not fit the colonial stereotype the Chairman was looking for. He asked questions like, if I had a white dinner jacket. He also wanted to know if I would be comfortable attending receptions at the Governor's Residence. My answers did not impress him so after about ten minutes, he informed me that they could not offer me a position. He encouraged me to apply again next year. I said that I would not likely apply again because I was not planning to be without a job for a year, even if I had to dig ditches. I had been brought up with a strong feeling of responsibility that a man must provide for his family.

At that point, one of the members of the interview board asked me, "Would you be interested in working in South America?"

I replied, "Yes Sir. I need a job. My wife is expecting our first child in November, and I would work anywhere."

This gentleman asked several more questions about my attitude towards working in the bush under adverse conditions. I said that I had worked for a year as a laborer in the forest in Hungary and that I always helped my father working on the farm.

The chairman, who obviously did not like me, intercepted and said, "Thank you Mr. Hegyi. We will notify you of our decision in due course."

As I traveled back to Edinburgh, I was sure that I did not get the job. I was surprised, therefore, when a few weeks later, I received a letter from the Department of Technical Cooperation of the Colonial Office, offering me a job as Assistant Conservator of Forests in British Guiana, South America.

Prior to going to British Guiana, I attended a six-week training course at the Directorate of Overseas Surveys in

Tolworth. The course was on aerial photo interpretation and forest surveys. Mr. R.G. Miller was in charge of my training, and on the first day we discovered that I did not have stereoscopic vision. Mr. Miller suggested that I go to see an Optometrist to be tested because aerial photo interpretation requires stereoscopic vision. The Optometrist found that I was short sighted with the left eye, which was also lazy and needed to be focused. When the Optometrist found out that my job depended on stereoscopic vision, he spent a lot of time helping me to train the left eye with the help of a monocle.

I practiced most of the night with a pocket stereoscope. Next morning at the office, I placed the monocle on the stereoscope to try to focus and by the afternoon, I was able to see stereoscopically. I went to Mr. Miller with the good news. He gave me a set of air photos and asked me to measure the height of trees with a parallax bar. I was able to give him a good estimate. As he went to check it out, he couldn't see himself stereoscopically, which made him really confused. We realized that my monocle had been left on the stereoscope. This gave Mr. Miller a good chuckle.

I was now trained to start my first professional job.

Into the Amazon Rain Forests

I was booked to leave for British Guiana on the 17th of November. I had time to get back to Edinburgh after my prost graduate training, pack my limited wardrobe and talk to my unborn child that I would like to be there when he comes into this world. He did not seem to want to cooperate. It was heart-wrenching, but I had to leave my family and go to Liverpool to sail on a cargo ship called Arakaka.

This was a unique experience. There were only twenty-one passengers on board. We became a closely knit group of fun-loving people. I was lucky to be accepted by the crew and made good friend with Sparks, the Communications Officer. I was expecting a telegraph in Hungarian as soon as our first child was born. The telegraph was to announce the baby's arrival and inform me as whether it was a boy or a girl. The purpose for sending it in Hungarian was that I would not have to buy a round of drinks on the occasion of becoming a father. I received the telegraph on November 19th.

Sparks asked me to translate: "What does it say?"

I was so excited that I told him, "My wife gave birth to a boy." That was it! I had to buy a round of drinks as we celebrated the happy occasion. Fortunately, drinks were cheap on the boat since there were no taxes to be paid to any government.

We arrived in Georgetown on Tuesday, December 4th 1961. Mr. Jeffrey Phillips, the Deputy Conservator of Forests, met me and took me to a guest house on Murray Street. This was only a walking distance from the office of the Forestry Department on Kingston Road, so it was really convenient because I had no money to buy a car or even a bicycle.

Next morning, I went to the office at 8 a.m. to report to Mr. Dow, the Conservator of Forests. When I walked into his office, I recognized him to be the person who asked me in London if I wanted to work in South America. He greeted me with a big smile, making me feel very comfortable about my first professional job. Mr. Dow did an excellent job with my orientation. He informed me that Mr. Tom Reese, who was also part of the interview panel, would be arriving shortly to train me on how to lead expeditions into the jungle. My co-workers helped me to rent a furnished house in Georgetown, which I took possession of on February 1st, 1962. Mr. Phillips was most helpful in this regard, offering to help me hire domestic help. I said that I did not need any. He argued that it would be considered by the local people as being selfish that I was not willing to share my income. I relented and we hired an Amerindian domestic help, Lena, for BG$30 per month plus room and board. Lena had a three-year-old daughter, Lisa. She was happy for the opportunity to work. She stayed with us during the entire three years that I was in British Guiana.

The political situation in British Guiana around that time was rather turbulent. The governing party was the Peoples Progressive Party (PPP) lead by Dr. Cheddi Jagan, a U.S. educated dentist of East Indian descent. The main opposition party was the Peoples National Congress (PNC), lead by Forbes Burnham, who represented the people of African descent. The other opposition party was the United Force (UF) lead by Peter D'Aguiar of Portuguese descent, who was for the big business interests. D'Aguiar owned the brewery, was connected to the Right Wing religious groups and controlled the local paper, the Chronicle.

My wife and son arrived in Georgetown on February 14th, 1962. I was excited to see my son for the first time. When they walked off the boat, Audrey handed Michael, named after my grandfather, over to me. Within minutes I had a warm and wet feeling. Michael did not have diapers on and he had decided to christen me. Audrey laughed and told me this was payback for not being there when Michael was born.

After collecting the luggage, we went to our rented house in a Forestry Department van. Audrey was surprised that we had domestic help. I explained to her the circumstances and she was pleased especially when she saw the great meal that Lena had prepared for the first dinner in their new home.

On February 15th, Mr. Phillips drove us around Georgetown and we walked along the famous sea wall. Audrey and I were excited about living in the tropics, seeing the palm trees, experiencing the warm climate and the tropical showers. It was unfortunate that the political climate made us very nervous because of the escalating disturbances.

On February 16th, the riots started. Opposition activity began very early on the morning of Friday 16 February in Water Street. Leaders and supporters of the UF encouraged people gathered there to go to the Parade Ground where D'Aguiar would address them. While that meeting was going on a small crowd gathered outside the electricity plant in Kingston and they threw stones and bottles at the windows of the building.

Journey to the Big World

My wife and I watched from the balcony of our rented home as looters took away furniture and other items. This was a new experience for us. We were almost having second thoughts about living in British Guiana, especially with a young baby. However, in a few days, the city seemed to return to *normal* and we were gradually adjusting to our new environment. Michael was especially enjoying the tropical climate.

In March 1962, Mr. Tom Reese arrived from the Department of Technical Cooperation, London, to train me on how to lead expeditions into the jungle and jungle survival. When he stepped off the ship, I recognized him as a person who was also on my interview panel. He was the former Conservator of Forests in Nigeria, a very kind Englishman who observed tradition in a rather original manner. He was there for three months and provided further training in aerial photo interpretation in the office, as well as training in the bush.

In early 1963, we moved into a furnished Government house at 252 Thomas Street, Georgetown, which was formerly the residence of the Chief Justice. The house had two stories, each level being self-contained. We had the first level and above us lived Professor Morrison Sharp and his wife.

Journey to the Big World

Picture 10. Mike and I while visiting the Botanical Gardens in Georgetown.

Picture 11. Living in Georgetown (left to right) Mr. Reese, Mr. Dow and Mr. Phillips

Picture 12. Lina, Michael and Lisa

Dr. Sharp was head of the History Department at the newly established University of British Guiana and was a U.S.

citizen with liberal views. He had left the U.S. because his academic career was ruined in the early 1950s by Senator Joseph McCarthy's persecutions of academics who had liberal views. Dr. Sharp and I had many discussions involving politics. He knew that I was anti-Communist. He was very interested to learn about life under Socialism and Communism. As we compared notes, we realized that people with extreme views on the Right, as well as on the Left were the cause of many sufferings.

As a Roman Catholic, I was disturbed to hear that it had been a Roman Catholic priest who had come up with the idea that McCarthy should begin a campaign against Communist subversives working in the Democratic administration. So many careers had been ruined, so many lives shattered by McCarthy in the name of righteousness, which was politically motivated and self-serving. I told Morrison that Communists did similar type of persecutions of those who were considered reactionaries. The damage was equally brutal.

Dr. Sharp said that he was part of a think tank who met every Saturday afternoon at the Tower Hotel to discuss world affairs. The leader of the group was Professor Lancelot Hogben, the new Vice Chancellor and Principal of the University of British Guiana. On occasions, Dr. Cheddi Jagan and Janet Jagan also attended the meetings. Because of my experience with life under Communism, I was invited to attend these meetings and argue against the Pro-Leftist views that some of the group members sympathized with. I was also asked to drive Prof. Lancelot to the meetings, which I considered a real honor.

The group was interested to hear about the cruelty of Communist officials, although someone always managed to draw a parallel situation caused by Right Wing extremists and the clergy. I found that the American born, Janet Jagan, was more of a Marxist than her husband, Cheddi. As I came to know the Jagans, I came to understand that both the John F. Kennedy and Harold McMillan governments had made a mistake by backing the opposition, especially Burnham, against the PPP.

While Dr. Jagan's meeting with President Kennedy in Washington could have led to a cordial relationship, it was the visit of Arthur Schlesinger, U.S. Secretary of State, to British Guiana that caused the problem for the Jagans. Schlesinger concluded after his visit that Dr. Jagan's heart was with the Communist world, and that, although all alternatives to Dr. Jagan were just as terrible, Schlesinger also felt that if Mr. Burnham could commit himself to a multi-racial policy, an independent British Guiana under his leadership would cause the U.S. fewer problems than one under Dr. Jagan.

History has, in my opinion, proven this to be a major miscalculation. Schlesinger only saw the charming side of Burnham. I was sitting with some friends at the next table to where Burnham was drinking with his buddies and I saw a sight that was frightening. I heard him say with such anger, "When I get to power..."

On one of the expeditions, I was visited at my base camp by a British Army Officer, Lt. John Foster. He had a camp in the Bartica Triangle about five miles from where I was. He was set up in the former residence of the regional manager of a lumber company called BG Timbers. His camp had a fridge and stove and indoor plumbing, which was a great luxury at that time in the bush.

One day, John invited me to go into the town of Bartica with him to get some supplies. He said that I could stay in his camp that evening. He had some cold beer, so I agreed to go with him. We jumped into his Land Rover (he was driving) and we were in Bartica in about three hours. We played some pool, bought supplies and had a nice meal, then headed back to his camp. About half way there, it started to get dark. John asked me to load one of the rifles and be ready in case we met some wild animals. Well, it happened shortly after, as we came around the bend, a tapir blocked the road and would not move. John blew the horn, but nothing happened. The animal was stuck in the headlights, frozen in spot, just looking in the direction of our vehicle. I let a few shots off in the air to try to scare her away, but it would not move. Then, suddenly she started to scratch the ground with the front right foot, ready to charge. Both John and I fired at the animal. It was now a matter of our survival. The tapir had been known to turn over a Land Rover. We decided not to take a chance. After a few shots, the animal fell to the ground and we started to walk towards it. Suddenly, the tapir stood up and charged us. We ran back to the Land Rover, I just managed to get in the door when the animal caught up with me, damaging the door on my side. John was by that time behind the wheel, yelling: "Are you in?"

I yelled back, "Yes, let's get the hell out of here."

Journey to the Big World

We drove off and made it safely to his camp. In the morning, we returned with some of his soldiers and found the tapir lying on the side of the road, dead. I felt so sick when the soldiers found a young one inside, also dead. After that, I would not lift a gun against a wild animal for the rest of my stay in Guyana and even now, I am against hunting animals.

The expedition was completed in early November. When I returned to Georgetown, I finished my report and started to pack my belongings. My wife and son were already in Edinburgh, Scotland, staying with her parents. As part of my contract, I was given six months paid leave and a trip back to Scotland.

Mr. Dow said that he would be happy to have me for another three years on contract. He suggested that I think about it and let him know in a couple of months. I shipped my stuff (we had no furniture, just clothes) back to Edinburgh on December 1st, and moved in to the Tower Hotel while I waited for a flight out.

Getting out of Georgetown was not easy. There was a general strike again and the Atkinson Airport was shut down. On December 2nd, some friends invited me to a party where I met some Canadians from the High Commission. They suggested that I visit Toronto on my way back to Scotland because Canada was looking for people with college degrees in forestry. The next day I went the Canadian High Commission and obtained a ten-day visitor's visa to travel through Canada. Now, I was on standby, waiting for a flight out.

On December 4th, I was having a drink in the bar, when a former neighbor, Miss. DeFreitas, came by to say hello. She was an airline hostess with Air France and I asked her to help me get to Trinidad. She said that on the next day she was flying to Trinidad with some people who were allowed out by the strikers. She suggested that I travel with her to the airport. That way, the picketers would let me through. On December 5th, I climbed on a scooter behind Miss DeFreitas, put my small suitcase in between us and headed to the airport. Miss DeFreitas was wearing her uniform so we were able to get through the picket line. I already had my airline ticket from British Airways, a full fare, so it was accepted for the portion from Georgetown to Port of Spain. I checked into a hotel next to the airport, and then went back to the airport to try to sort out my flights. I took my full fare ticket issued by British Airways to Air Canada and asked them if I could use that to fly to Scotland via Toronto. They were happy to accept it and gave me a new ticket that allowed me to visit both Toronto and Montreal before going back to Glasgow.

While I enjoyed the three years in British Guiana and I found the people very nice and friendly, the political unrest was not conducive for me to consider another three-year tour. Even some of my local colleagues were looking at leaving Georgetown for a safer place to live. I was determined to try my best to find a job in Canada where my son would have a better future. I had survived the jungle and the riots, but didn't want to push my luck for another three years.

Integrating into Canada

After landing at Malton Airport (now the Toronto Pearson International Airport) in Toronto, I went to look for a taxi to take me to downtown. I had no hat and was wearing a light suit, raincoat and regular shoes. The outside temperature was -30°C and reality check hit me that I needed to buy warmer clothes.

I climbed into the taxi and asked the driver to recommend a good central hotel to stay in Toronto. He said the best and most central one was the Royal York.

I said, "OK, take me there." I had no reservation, but when I asked at the registration desk, there was no problem securing a room. This was Sunday evening, December 6, 1964. The next morning, I started to make phone calls to the Ontario Ministry of Natural Resources. I managed to arrange an appointment with Mr. Art Herridge, Head of the Silviculture Branch in Downsview. He advised me to take the subway to Queens Park where I could catch the government car that goes to Downsview every hour, on the hour. Mr. Herridge said that he would call the driver to expect me at 1 p.m. I arrived at Mr. Herridge's office at about 1:30 p.m. The interview lasted about half an hour. Mr Herridge offered me a job, but said that I would have to start at the bottom of the ladder. I said that was no problem. I would look forward to working my way up the ladder.

He said, "Welcome to the Forest Resources Inventory unit of OMNR." He then escorted me to the FRI unit and introduced me to Victor Zsillinsky, who was the forester in charge of the Aerial Photo Interpretation Unit, and was originally from Hungary.

Victor was most helpful in briefing me about life in Canada. We called the Immigration Officer and I suggested that since I had a job, there is no point in my returning to Scotland. The Immigration Officer said that I still needed to apply for Landed Immigrant Status.

I said, "Okay, where do I sign up?"

He said it was not that simple, even though I had a job. I would have to apply from the country of origin, in this case Hungary.

"Well," I said. "That is problematic. I escaped about three hours before I was going to be shot. Do I have another option?"

After some discussions, the Immigration Officer suggested that since I had a B.Sc. from Edinburgh University, I was married to a British subject, had a son who was born in Scotland, I would qualify as a Scottish immigrant. Consequently, I had to return to Scotland after all, where I then applied for Landed Immigrant Status in Canada.

The Canadian Immigration Office was in Glasgow. Upon arriving home, I immediately took the train from Edinburgh. I filled out all of the papers, and then had an interview. The Immigration Officer was very cooperative. He reassured me that I would not have any problems being accepted. I had to get a medical, including a chest x-ray. They found a spot on my lungs which threatened to block my immigration to Canada. I had to go to a specialist to get clearance that I had no tuberculosis. That took a couple of weeks of nervous waiting until I received my clearance. I finally obtained Landed Immigrant Status at the beginning of February. I was now allowed to work in Canada.

On Sunday February 13th 1965, I boarded a British Airways flight from Prestwick, Scotland, heading to Toronto. All passengers spoke with a Scottish accent and I was like a misfit on the flight, officially a Scottish immigrant with a Hungarian accent. When we were going though Immigration at Toronto Airport, even the Immigration Officer spoke with a Scottish accent. He looked at my papers, and, seeing the name Hegyi (I should have changed it to McHegyi), he asked, "Are ye from Glasgow?"

I answered, "Augh no man, I am from Edinburgh, Morningside." (In Edinburgh, most of the English settled in the Morningside subdivision).

He said, "Away ye go." As I walked away, I heard him say to his colleague, "We get all kinds you know."

Now that I was a Landed Immigrant in Canada, I started to be more fugal with my money. I had a savings of about $3,000 Canadian, which had to last until I received my first pay cheque.

Canada was quite different from the places where I had lived before. During my time in Britain, I always felt like a foreigner. Although people were very nice, helpful, even friendly, and the country gave me an education, I still didn't feel like I belonged there. Marrying a Scottish girl didn't change what happened when I opened my mouth and the secret was out that I was a foreigner. For example, when people realized that I graduated with a B.Sc. degree from Edinburgh University, the response usually was, "Well, haven't you done well for yourself?" I am sure this was meant in the best of spirits, but I always felt the unspoken part of the response: "for a foreigner".

I never considered British Guiana a home. I just worked there for three years. I met some very nice people, but I was an expatriate. I viewed Canada as a possible home where I wanted to spend the rest of my life. In the 1960's Canada was cosmopolitan and basically everybody, except the First Nations was a foreigner, some having arrived recently, while others dated back a few generations. Talking about the *old country* was quite common and acceptable. One could do so without feeling labeled.

First, I stayed at the Holiday Inn on Dufferin (close to Wilson Avenue), from where I could go to the office by bus, which was at Downsview. Victor Zsillinsky helped me find a two-bedroom apartment on Keele Street (just north of Wilson), which was within walking distance of the office.

Next came the challenge of buying furniture. I was told by my co-workers that it was important to establish credit in Canadian society. Roy Gilbert, a very helpful co-worker suggested that I should buy the furniture at the government employee's store called GEMS. He drove me there, I selected just the essential furniture for a two-bedroom apartment for a cost of $600. It consisted of a double bed, a single bed for my son, the cheapest kitchen table with four chairs, a chesterfield and an arm chair.

Having made my selection, I then went to the credit department and filled out an application form for credit. When the credit representative interviewed me, she said that it could not be approved because I had no previous credit and had only been in the job for a week. However, I talked her into approving it on the condition that I would pay it off in full before they delivered the furniture to my apartment. She said this was a most unusual procedure, but she agreed and I was on my way to establish credit rating in Canada. For a year, I used this system, after which the credit department notified me that I could just pay the monthly minimum from then on.

My wife and son joined me on March 2nd 1965, by which time I had the apartment furnished, in a fashion. I was doing well at work and, although the condition for taking the job was that I would start at the bottom, by the time the field season started in June, I was promoted to Party Chief, in charge of mapping the forest stands of the Sault Ste. Marie Management Unit. In April, I received my Canadian driver's license, using Roy's car so I was able to drive the crew around during the field work.

Journey to the Big World

Picture 13. Victor and I became personal friends.

On December 15, 1965, my wife gave birth to a beautiful little girl, whom we named Jennifer. I was so excited when the doctor told me it was a little girl that I dropped my wrist watch on the marble floor of the hospital which then broke into many pieces.

Picture 14. Jennifer and I

In early 1966, we managed to buy a used car, a 1964 Dodge. This car had the habit of stalling in the rain. One afternoon, as I was driving home from work around 4:30 p.m., going north on Keele Street, just before making a left hand turn to our parking lot, my car stalled. The driver behind me was very impatient and kept honking his horn. Since that didn't help the situation, I climbed out of my car, went back to talk to him. As he lowered his window, I said to him, "Excuse me, sir. That is my car there. It is stalled. I wonder if you could help me by going there and start it while I stay here and honk your horn."

Well, he didn't have a sense of humor. He started addressing me in a not very nice language. He was cognizant of the fact that I was an immigrant and even had some colorful adjectives to me. However, when he started to describe me in terms of certain parts of the anatomy that were rather private, I thought it best that I return to my car, which fortunately then started.

In June 1966, I was offered a job with the Canadian Forestry Service. There was a shortage of researchers who were specializing in biometrics and my job offer was conditional on my willingness to go back to the university to study for a Master's degree. This was an opportunity of a lifetime and I eagerly accepted it. I attended classes during the academic year of 1967-68. I was given half-salary from the Government of Canada and, based on my marks during the first term exams, I won a scholarship which made my take home pay almost as much as the regular pay was. I completed the academic requirements for a M.Sc. degree in June 1968. After that I was transferred from Toronto to Sault Ste. Marie to the Great Lakes Forest Research Centre.

We managed to buy a modest home for $10,500 in Sault Ste. Marie in June 1968 (because now I had a well-established credit rating). This was a starter home, single story with crawling place underneath. It had a large kitchen, two bedrooms, a living room and an attached garage. It was in a run-down condition, badly needed painting and some repairs. I decided to do the painting myself with some coaching from Bert Diboll who lived across the street. Painting the outside of the house was no problem. It was summer time and I was wearing only a pair of shorts which became garish-looking, advertising the different paints that I was supposed to put on the side of the house. My body was also covered with paint and cleaning it with turpentine proved to be more difficult than I had initially imagined.

I also painted the rooms inside, but by this time I learned to put most of the paint on the walls rather than on myself. I just had one little accident when I put my foot into the tray of paint as I stepped off the ladder. It would have still been alright if I hadn't made two more steps on the carpet before reaching the newspapers that were supposed to cover the entire floor area.

Picture 15. Michael and Jennifer in the backyard

Our starter home had a large backyard with lawn for the children to play on. I even made a small vegetable garden, growing lettuce, tomato, peppers, carrots and potatoes. The children were enjoying the house with a backyard a lot more than the apartment that they were used to in Toronto. They made friends with the children in the neighborhood and playing baseball in the backyard was a popular pastime in the afternoons and evenings.

In the fall of 1968, Audrey found a job as a lab technician at Great Lakes Forest Research Centre. This became a turning point in our lives. She and her boss, Michael Larsen, developed a relationship. As a result, we had a difficult family life during the winter and spring of 1969.

I completed the thesis for my M.Sc. degree in the spring of 1969 and graduated in June of that year. Mr. Bud Smithers, the Director-General of Great Lakes Research Centre, who had recruited me into the Federal Civil Service, offered to send me to the University of British Columbia in Vancouver to study for a PhD degree in computer simulation modeling. I visited UBC in July and was told that, based on my marks and thesis work at the University of Toronto, I would be accepted. There was even a good chance of even getting a scholarship to complement the half salary offered by the Research Centre.

When I returned from UBC, Audrey informed me that Michael Larsen had left his wife and three children. He had rented a cottage and asked her to move in with him. Discussions that followed afterwards were very difficult, especially in the light of the two young children and my postgraduate study plans.

Audrey was dating Larsen two to three times a week in the evenings while I stayed home with the children, trying to come to terms with the family crisis. One evening, after the children went to bed, I went to their bedroom and looked at them sleeping with complete innocence, not realizing what was going on in their little lives.

I cried for about an hour in total despair, not knowing what to do. When Audrey came home that evening, she informed me that she had decided to move in with Larsen. The complication was that the cottage was in the country and there was no room for the children to stay with her. I then jumped at the opportunity by saying that the children would stay with me. I would look after their schooling and they could spend the holidays with her.

The following day, I went to see Bud Smithers and told him of the family situation. I informed him that I had decided to look after the children, so I would have to decline his offer of supporting me for PhD studies. Bud was a devoted family man, had tears in his eyes when he gave me a big hug and told me that he would have made the same decision in my place.

Audrey moved out to live with Larsen in August 1969 and I started a new life as a single parent. Since the divorce proceedings started in September 1969, I was put under the watchful eye of the Children's Aid Society. After all, in 1969 it was unusual for a single father to go for the custody of two young children. Several times, a representative of Children's Aid came with a white glove to check if there was any dust on the furniture. I used to get up at 4 a.m. to clean the house, scrub the floors and get the children ready for the babysitter, Mrs. Jean Diboll, who lived across the road. After work, I would make supper and play with the children. After they went to bed, I did other chores such as the laundry and dishes. Just before Christmas 1969, I brought my parents out from Hungary to help me with the children.

My parents only spoke Hungarian so I was nervous about the challenges that they would face when changing planes in Frankfurt and also in Toronto. When they arrived in Sault Ste. Marie, I asked my mother how they knew when to change gates. She said that they just looked at the ticket that indicated the airline that they were flying with and, about an hour before boarding, they went over to the airline counter and she started to cry. An attendant would come and offer them some tea and watch over them until it was ready to proceed to the gate. After that, someone always escorted them right to the gate and onto the plane at boarding time.

Picture 16. My parents with the kids

After the Children's Aid representative met my mother, she did not come back to check on me anymore. After all, there was now a woman in the house. It is interesting to note that my mother was from a small village in Hungary, her home had dirt floors, the toilet facilities consisted of an outhouse, and there was no running water. She was not used to the hygiene that I practiced, but she fit the expectation of the Children's Aid Society to look after children: she was a woman! And of course, I didn't complain. I was grateful to have the opportunity of looking after my children without the surprise visits from Children's Aid.

My divorce was finalized in January 1970. Since Audrey did not attend the hearings, I was given full custody of the children. However, I told her that I would honor our earlier agreement about the children spending the holidays with her.

As a single parent, I joined Parents Without Partners (PWP) and took Michael and Jennifer to children's activities, such as bowling and birthday parties. In November 1969, I met Rose McKinnon who had a seven-year-old son named Randy. We organized a lot of activities together. The children were getting on well and so did we. I even become Public Relations Director for PWP.

Rose and I shared the same values in several key areas. We both were focused on the happiness of our children and in the importance of friendship that was based on kindness and support for each other. Around the middle of January, Rose invited me to attend the wedding of one of her cousins in the Anglican Church. During the ceremony, my mind started to wonder about having a relationship with Rose. It was similar to what my parents had, going to church on Sundays and leading a peaceful life. I was impressed with the warmness of the Anglican priests towards family life. It showed an understanding that was based on practical experience.

After the ceremony, Rose and I discussed the desirability of introducing the children to religious education. Although both of us were christened and baptized as Roman Catholics, due to a number of personal reasons, neither of us had married previously in the Roman Catholic Church. Rose was first married in an Anglican Church. I had been married in the Presbyterian Church. We started to check out both denominations to see which one was going to be most suitable to provide an education for our children. After attending a service at a Presbyterian Church, we met the minister, Rev. Peter McKeage, who was very sympathetic to our situation of two divorced single parents supporting each other in bringing up children. Peter was married and had three children in the same age ranges as our three were.

We started to attend the Presbyterian Church regularly and the children were enrolled in Sunday school. I even volunteered to help with Sunday school. After some discussions with Peter, he assigned me to teach the senior class with focus on religious philosophy, origin of religion and an understanding of other denominations. I did a lot of research on the different religious denominations and saw a lot of good in each of them, but at the same time I found that some of them were often self-serving. My approach to teaching the advanced class was focusing on the positive side of religious beliefs and lifestyles.

Rose and I were gradually developing a relationship with cautious optimism. We both agreed that a condition for us to consider having a life together was that the children would get along with each other, as well as be comfortable in a family unit. We decided to experiment and allow the children opportunities to interact with us and each other in different situations. On a Friday night, Randy would stay overnight at my house and on Saturday night Michael and Jennifer would sleep over at Rose's apartment. Jennifer found this a little confusing and asked why I would not stay over at Rose's or why Rose would not sleep over at our house. We explained to her that we would do that only when we were married.

Our friendship grew into love. We decided to get married, provided that we had the children's approval. I first talked to Michael and Jennifer about getting married to Rose and they were in favor. Rose received Randy's approval, as well. We sat down together and discussed our new lifestyles. With the help of Rev. Peter McKeage, we planned a very private wedding at the church for June 30th, 1970, with only immediate family and close friends attending. My neighbor, Bill Kidd, was the Best Man and Rose's friend, Mildred Bebee, was the Maid of Honor. Rose bought a beautiful white pantsuit for Jennifer and the boys were decked out in a suit with white shirt and tie.

Michael and Jennifer lead the wedding party up the aisle, and Randy gave his mother away. Peter performed a wonderful ceremony. It was based on our dedication to the children and the desire to merge the two families in a warm, family environment. As we came out of the church after the ceremony, most of us were still kind of teary eyed. Jennifer broke the silence by saying in a loud voice, "Oh good Rose. Now you can sleep with my Daddy because you are married." That brought out laughter even from the usually serious Rev. Peter McKeage!

Picture 17. I married Rose and the children participated.

In early July 1970, my mother returned to Hungary (my father returned in March). Rose and I took the children to a cottage in Chaplaeu for two weeks. I was doing field work on a forest fertilization research project in Chaplaeu. The children really enjoyed the outdoors and swimming in the lake. In August, Jennifer and Michael went to visit their mother and, in September, the three children started attending the same school just walking distance from our house.

In the summer of 1971, I became very ill. It felt like a slipped disc. The pain in my back was intense and I could only walk with the help of two canes. Dr. White at the Sault Ste. Marie Health Care Centre diagnosed it as Marie-Strumpell Spondylitis or Ankylosing Spondylitis. He drew a diagram of the spine and pelvic bones to show me where the disease was going to fuse the bones. Dr. White also showed me pictures of people who ended up being bent over after the spine fused, and said that it was wise to be prepared. He informed me that I could end up in a wheelchair within a year as a worst case scenario. Dr. White prescribed indocid (indomethacin), which belongs to the class of medications known as *nonsteroidal anti-inflammatories* (NSAIDs). I was taking three pills a day, attended physiotherapy regularly and, with the help of two canes, was able to walk to the car so that Rose could drive me to work.

Just when things were going well, life presented me another crisis. By now, I was getting to be an expert in turning crisis into new opportunities. First, I survived losing my country and managed to get an education in the west. Then, I survived the jungles and the riots in South America. The divorce had been devastating, but it taught me the importance of being a parent and that looking after children is not a chore, but a wonderful privilege. Now, I was facing the health crisis and the possibility of not being able to walk again.

In order to prepare for a life in a wheelchair, I became increasingly involved in computer programming. I had to face the possibility of not being able to do the field work anymore. Fortunately, I had taken Computer Science as part of my Master of Science course work, so I had the foundation to build upon. With a new focus in my research work, I started to build computer software models that could simulate the growth of trees and forest stands. The software languages that I used were FORTRAN and APL.

Gradually, indocid was helping to ease the inflammation of the joints and I was able to walk without much pain, as long as I watched my diet and was taking the medication. I was determined to overcome this new hurdle and started to research a new subject: mind over matter. I found that a positive attitude helped me with my newly acquired handicap almost as much as the prescribed medication. I did a lot of physiotherapy and gradually I was able to walk without a cane.

My computer simulation research work was getting some recognition among computer vendors. IBM was very supportive in giving me access to the timesharing system in Toronto that I accessed with a remote terminal through the telephone. Ian Sharpe, CEO of I. P. Sharp Associates, the suppliers of APL computer programming language, invited me to set up my simulation model on their main frame computer using APL. I went to visit them in Toronto and, after seeing the possible advantages of this new programming language, I agreed to try it out. In a highly cooperative spirit, I was given a free account for three months and the loan of a computer terminal which looked like a medium size suitcase. It had just a keyboard, the electronics, and the wires to connect it to a television which was used as the monitor.

As I was trying to get on the airplane with this terminal, the airline staff spent a lot of time examining it and finally they let me take it onboard. I was the last person to get on the plane and there was just one aisle seat left. I managed to put the computer terminal under the seat in front of me, then said hello to the lady who was sitting at the window seat next to me. We started to talk after we were airborne and she asked me what was in that unusual looking suitcase. I proudly told her that it was a computer terminal. I explained to her briefly that I was a research scientist and what I was going to do with it. She looked impressed. I then asked her what she did for a living. She said that she was a writer. She had just finished a book called *On Death and Dying*, based on interviews with patients who were diagnosed with terminal illnesses. I told her it was pretty gutsy for a writer to take on such a subject.

She then smiled and said, "Actually, I am also a medical doctor." I was interested in the subject matter and we ended up having a good discussion about people's reactions. She explained the five stages patients go through when they learn that they are terminally ill:

Denial and isolation: "not me, it cannot be true"

Anger: "why me?"

Bargaining: "yes me...but"

Depression: "yes me"

Acceptance: "it's OK"

I said that, while I appreciated her research findings, from personal experience, I could honestly say that death can also be a welcome alternative when living is becoming unbearable. In that case, the five-stage-theory did not cover all of the stages. It is not a question as to whether or not you accept death. You may just want to reject living. I had experienced that feeling when I was crawling over the border strip that was expected to have landmines buried underneath the surface.

She said that she appreciated my input to her research findings. She then introduced herself as Elizabeth Kübler Ross. Since I was only reading technical books around that time, her name didn't mean anything to me. She invited me to the lecture that she was giving in the Plummer Hospital that evening, gave me her business card and informed me that it would allow me access to the lecture.

Rose was waiting for me with a car at the airport in Sault Ste. Marie. We offered Elizabeth a lift to her hotel. After supper, I decided to go to the lecture. Elizabeth had already started her talk when I tried to sneak into the back of the auditorium without being noticed. Elizabeth saw me, stopped the lecture and said, "Hi Frank, I am so pleased that you accepted my invitation to listen to my talk."

At that point, everybody looked at me like I was somebody important. During the lecture, she dealt with the five stages patients faced when they learned that they were terminally ill. She said that during her clinical research, these stages were consistently confirmed, although as she was coming to Sault Ste. Marie, she met a gentleman on the plane who challenged the concept of five phases.

"Frank Hegyi, who is in the audience, said that my findings were incomplete. There is another stage, where it is not a matter of accepting death, but rather one rejects living."

I think I must have turned ten shades of red as people looked at me. After the lecture, I had a chance to talk to Elizabeth. I apologized for not knowing who she was. She smiled and gave me an autographed copy of her book. She was leaving the Sault early next morning. Her flight was at 6 a.m. from Sault, Michigan. I offered to give her a lift which she accepted. After that I read her book and we even exchanged Christmas cards for a few years.

I enjoyed the transition from Field Forester to Research Scientist and became quite successful in developing computer simulation models. Research Scientists were expected to publish in referred journals, so I started publishing the results of my work.

In 1973, my focus shifted to accessing mainframe computers through timesharing. I upgraded to a state-of-the-art computer terminal and was accessing both the IBM and the IP Sharp mainframe computers in Toronto from Sault Ste. Marie through dialup telephone. The IBM Customer Service Representative encouraged me to demonstrate this new technology to other scientists. Cambrian College had a modern lecture theatre with four televisions suspended from the ceiling and wired to a central feed. We managed to interface my computer terminal with this central feed to display the output of my simulation model on the TV screens. In addition to the scientists in the Sault, the Research Centre invited scientists from other research centers and universities.

I was getting a little bit nervous when they showed me the list of people who had accepted the invitation. It included Dr. Earl Stone, Editor of the Forest Science Journal, Dr. Al Leaf, a professor from Syracuse University, Dr. Terry Honer, Manager of the Computer Simulation Program of the Canadian Forest Service in Victoria, B.C., and Denis Glew, Manager of the Computer Simulation Program on Forest Planning with the B.C.

Forest Service. Ian Sharpe and IBM hosted a reception the evening before the demonstration and I was getting even more nervous as I listened to the expectations of these high-ranking people. After a couple of stiff drinks, I reconciled myself to my fate, realizing that the next day, I would either make it big or I would have to start looking for a new job.

The next morning, my staff and I had a quick dress rehearsal of the demonstration. The show began. In the background, we played classical music during the demonstration. The dial-up process was accompanied by *Sabre Dance* by Khachaturian, and when we connected the music switched to *Hungarian Dance Number 5* by Brahms. The music gradually faded away during the demonstration.

The program included specifying the criteria for the forest we were creating in terms of species (the species selected for the model was Jack Pine), number of trees per hectare, competition indices, and timeframe. The model showed a summary of stand characteristics at five year intervals, including the average diameter at breast height, basal area, the number of trees per hectare and the volume of merchantable timber per hectare. In addition, the model illustrated the stand structure at each interval through a schematic diagram which showed how we were growing the trees in the computer.

The demonstration lasted for an hour where the audience was given an opportunity of specifying new conditions for the model and actually visualizing the corresponding results. At the end of the show, we piped in the *Alleluia* chorus by Handel to indicate that the demonstration was complete according to expectations.

At this point in time, I was beginning to feel comfortable about Canada as my new home and my adopted country. I was very lucky that with the attitude of *mind over matter*, I had regained a hundred percent of my mobility, and with diet and regular exercise my crippling arthritis was under control.

Also, I was involved with the Kiwanis and was elected to be Governor of the Pacific North West.

Picture 18. Rose and I at a Kiwanis meeting after my Governor's installation

Return to the Old Country

My parents urged us to visit them in Hungary. Some of the people who left in 1956 had already returned to visit relatives and were free to return to their chosen country. We decided to go for a visit.

When we landed in Budapest and saw the soldiers with machine guns around the plane and inside the airport, I was having second thoughts about the visit. My sister, Annuska, and her husband, Tibor, were waiting for us at the airport, but I didn't recognize her at first. She had been eleven years old when I left Hungary. Since that time, I only saw pictures of her.

As we came out from the secure area, a young lady was staring at me. After a few minutes, she walked over and said, "I am waiting for my brother who is coming from Canada with three children. Since you are the only family arriving with three children, you must be my brother."

We shed some tears and composed ourselves before introducing the family. We decided to go for an espresso coffee to discuss the itinerary. The children were happy to find that coca cola was a popular drink in Hungary and desserts were especially sweet. Through the travel agent in Canada, I had reserved a rental car and both Rose and I had obtained international driver's licenses. While the family was enjoying the refreshments, my brother-in-law, Tibor, and I went to pick up a rental car.

When we returned, both Rose and Annuska were laughing. They appeared to be having such a great conversation even though they understood only a few words in each other's dialogue. I had to assume the task of being an interpreter for the rest of the trip.

It was after 3 o'clock in the afternoon that we started our journey from the airport through Budapest to our village in Nyögér. My brother-in-law was driving a car that he had borrowed from a cousin and I followed him with the rental car. It was a Russian car, a Fiat model called Zsiguli, with standard transmission. Driving that car through Budapest during the rush hour was quite a challenge. The trip to my parent's village took about five hours. It was almost 8 p.m. when we arrived at the house where I was born. Everything had changed so much. I actually missed our gate. This amused my sister to such an extent that she had to tell almost everybody in the village.

In Nyögér, we had many relatives and they kept coming until about 2 a.m. to say hello and have a drink of pálinka (prunes brandy). The relatives kept asking if living conditions were much better in Canada. I had to be very careful not to make any comment about that. The next morning we tried to sleep in, but neighbors started to drop in at 5 a.m. for a toast of pálinka. Of course, I only responded with a glass of milk, saying that I had to drive later on. This was understood because there was zero tolerance for alcohol in Hungary if you were driving.

We spent the morning walking around the fruit orchard and vineyard in the backyard and talking about how things had been before 1956. After lunch, we drove into the nearest town, Sárvár, where I had attended High School. We had to report to the nearest police station within twenty-four hours of arriving in

Hungary. Even after that, if we went for a visit that lasted more than twenty-four hours, we had to report to the nearest police station. After registering with the police, we went for a walk in Sárvár to see how much things had changed. I visited my old High School. Two of my former teachers were still there. They told me that my class had lost four students to the West during the Revolution.

Visiting relatives was very interesting. I had been eighteen years old when I left Hungary. That was eighteen years ago. Both the people and the landscape had changed to such an extent that I felt like a stranger in the land that was my birthplace. Even the language changed so much that as soon as I started to talk, they knew that I was a *foreigner*. I was frequently asked which country I came from. This was a very strange reception, especially coming from fellow Hungarians in the land of my birth.

My cousins, with whom I used to play as a youngster, had changed so much that I could not put names to the faces, which was embarrassing. They definitely had an advantage over me since they knew who I was. My sister offered little help. She actually enjoyed watching me being quizzed by a relative who would ask, "Do you remember my name?"

Instead of whispering the name to me, my sister would repeat the question, "Well, do you know the name?"

Still, I found it very nostalgic to meet the many relatives, especially from my mother's side. In particular, I found it interesting how the social dimensions had changed during the past eighteen years. In the late 1940s, my father's side of the family considered themselves the major land owners and my mother's side was looked down on for being *peasants* because they had only a few hectares of land that they cultivated with cows and oxen rather than with horses.

During Communism, my father's side of the family remained defiant to changes and consequently became poorer. They continued to live in houses with dirt floors, no inside pluming and running water, and the outhouses were equipped with newspapers rather than with user-friendly toilet paper. My mother's side of the family, on the other hand, became trades workers. They were able to build brick houses with indoor plumbing, wooden floors and modern appliances, including television.

A particularly disappointing part of the visit was the perception from my father's side of the family that those of us who were living in the West had trees that grew money. My sister was particularly focused on this. As soon as she found out that we were going to visit Hungary, she sent a list of presents that she wanted us to bring. These presents would have cost us much as our airfare if we were to buy them all.

While in Hungary, she never missed an opportunity of letting me know what other people were getting from relatives who were living in America. She even researched how I could send her husband, Tibor, a car through the international travel agency called IBUSZ. Tibor had a driver's license (being a bus driver) so he could drive my parents around. In fact, she rationalized that the car would not be so much for her family, but for my parents so I should seriously think about it. I owed that to my parents. I was getting increasingly disappointed with the strong pressure I was subjected to by my sister in terms of how much money and gifts that I should give to her.

One Saturday afternoon, I asked my sister if she and her husband would be our guests for dinner in Sárvár at a nice restaurant where we could listen to live gypsy music. She eagerly accepted the invitation. When we were seated in the restaurant, I told Annuska that I would order the meals. After all, I could still speak Hungarian. We all agreed to have the same meal, a real traditional gourmet dish called, *Gypsy steak*, which is fried steak with onions and spices, prepared like the gypsies would cook it over an open fire beside their caravans. It was very tasty. The leader of the band called Primás was making his way to our table, hoping for a generous tip from this foreigner. I started to order the meal. When I tried to say, "Gypsy steak," in Hungarian, the waiter couldn't hear me. I raised my voice and repeated my request. As an unfortunate coincidence, when I shouted the name of the meal, the Primás paused for a second. Everyone nearby could hear what I had ordered. As soon as I pronounced the name of the meal, I knew that I had made a mistake. I had confused it with a word which has a similar sound.

I should have said in Hungarian, "Cigány pecsenye." Mistakenly, I said: "Cigány pöcse." Well, Cigány means gypsy, pecsenye is steak, but pöcse means penis. I immediately corrected myself.

The Primás had a good sense of humor. As soon as I said the correct word, he said, "Thank God." This made everybody laughing uncontrollably. My sister particularly enjoyed this and by

Journey to the Big World

the end of next day, the entire village knew how I had butchered the Hungarian language.

Picture 19. We visited my relatives in Hungary.

Picture 20. Randy, Jennifer and Michael with their pet chickens.

Picture 21. My parents with their grandchildren.

One day I decided to drop in to visit the Forest Research Institute in Sárvár. I was received warmly by the Deputy Director, Dr. Lajos Halupa. He had read my article on the simulation model and was interested in knowing more about it. He asked me if I would make a presentation about my research work to some of the staff at the Institute. I agreed and we lined up a meeting for the following week in order to give me time to prepare.

The Board Room at the Institute looked over a park. On the other side of the park, I could see my old High School building. When the meeting began, Dr. Halupa introduced me, in Hungarian, as Mr. Hegyi, a visiting forest engineer from Canada who, fortunately for us, also speaks Hungarian. As I was looking out the window, I could see my old High School building. I suddenly felt a detachment from the country of my birth. This detachment deepened as I was trying to explain how my computer simulation model was constructed and what deliverables it offered. I did not know the technical terms in Hungarian, but fortunately one of the researchers had some knowledge of English and he could translate for me some of the key terminology from English to Hungarian. At the end of my presentation, we had a long technical discussion and in the meantime, someone called the University of Sopron, Forest Engineering Faculty. Consequently, I received an invitation to make a presentation there, too. In the next few days, I learned the technical terms in Hungarian and, by the time I was making a presentation in Sopron, I was almost speaking fluent Hungarian.

One day, I was invited for a drink at the home of Tibor Berkes, a former school mate who was an agricultural engineer and chairman of the collective farm in Nyögér. Tibor told me confidentially that he had helped my father out with the police when my father had returned from Canada in 1970. My father had been arrested by the police in Sárvár and interrogated about why my mother did not return with him. My father always had a sense of humor. He told the police that my mother couldn't return with him because she enrolled in a dancing school in Sault Ste. Marie and the lessons were to last until July, at which time she would return to Hungary.

The policeman in charge of the interrogation, not having a sense of humor, accused him that his wife was defecting and threatened to put him in jail until my mother returned. Since my father was employed at the collective farm in Nyögér, the police informed Tibor about this development. In addition to being chairman of the collective farm, Tibor was also Secretary of the local Communist Party, which earned him respect with the police. So Tibor went to Sárvár in his chauffeur-driven car, had my father released from jail, and drove him back to the village. He was still laughing about the idea of my mother being enrolled in a dancing school in Canada and wondered where my father had come up with such an that idea to humor the police.

While I was growing up in Hungary, the musical theatre always fascinated me, mainly the documentaries. I never had the opportunity to go to a live theatre in those days Now, I was determined to take in at least one show. One day when we were visiting Szombathely, a town that was about thirty kilometers from our village, I noticed that they were advertising a musical called *Baroness Maria*. I bought two tickets for the Saturday evening show. They were good seats, located in the middle of the fifth row.

On Saturday afternoon Rose asked me the typical question, "What is the dress code for the theatre?"

I advised her without checking with anybody. I suggested that she wear a long dress as I was going to put on a grey suit with a green velvet bow tie. I further qualified my advice with the statement that we should dress almost formal for the theatre to blend in with the audience and not be conspicuous.

When we arrived at the theatre, we were the only ones *dressed up*, except for an army officer who was wearing his uniform. In fact, most of the young affluent people were wearing American jeans! To make the situation even worse, as one elderly lady was sitting down in front of me, she noticed my velvet green bow tie. She turned around and asked if she could touch it because she thought that it looked so nice and smooth, that it had to be from America.

At that point, Rose commented with a chuckle, "So much for your idea of not being conspicuous."

The children really enjoyed the time that we spent at my parent's house where there were lots of fruit trees, vegetables in the garden and animals.

The four weeks that we spent in Hungary went fast. We were able to visit many of our close relatives. All too soon came the time to say goodbye with more tears, especially from my mother. We left Nyögér at 2 a.m. in order to catch an early morning flight with Air France to Paris. The flight was delayed for an hour. When it finally took off, I was beginning to shed some of the tension that I had been experiencing while visiting Hungary.

The ease of tension did not last long. We were in the air for only twenty minutes when the Captain announced that we were landing in Prague for an emergency stopover. We were ordered to deplane and were escorted into a waiting room by soldiers pointing machine guns at us. Inside the terminal, a rumor started circulating. There was talk that the soldiers were going to escort back to Budapest a former Hungarian freedom fighter who was visiting Hungary. I looked at Rose and said that they may be looking for me. Quietly I said goodbye to the children and told Rose to contact the Canadian Embassy in Paris as soon as she arrived.

We watched as a half dozen Czechoslovakian policemen enter the waiting room with machine guns, a picture in hand, and scrutinizing the passengers. They looked at me as we stood still, but they moved on and stopped at another passenger, handcuffed him and led him out of the room. We were escorted by the soldiers back to the plane and we proceeded on to France.

On the plane from Prague to Paris, I was reflecting on the visit to Hungary. In eighteen years, were there any real changes? The first real change that I noticed was that the dreaded Secret Police, the AVH had been disbanded. The regular police, however, still had an iron-fist control of the population. Food was more abundant in the stores and some of the basic articles such as cloths and home supplies were now available. Also, there was a change in Communist leadership at the grass-roots level. The uneducated party leaders were replaced by people who had at least a High School education or a University diploma. There were signs that changes were taking place slowly and the early terror and persecutions of the people had been slowly phased.

As we landed in Paris, I was very thankful that I had escaped Hungary in 1956 and was once again headed back to a free world. I had warm feelings towards Canada, my adopted country.

Journey to the Big World

To Succeed Professionally

After returning from Hungary, I was invited to apply for a job as Research Scientist at the Pacific Forest Research Centre in Victoria B.C. It was an opportunity to get a promotion and to move to a town which had a university that the children would be able to attend. Of course, the weather in Victoria was considered to be much better than the severe winters that we were used to in Sault Ste. Marie. I applied and was invited to go to Victoria for an interview. Dr. Terry Honer, who was present at the computer simulation demonstration in Sault Ste. Marie, presided over the interview. He was the Program Manager for the position that I had applied for. Luck was with me again. I was offered the job, accepted it and the family was excited to face this new opportunity.

We sold the house in Sault Ste. Marie and bought a new one in Victoria. The Government paid for the move of our household possessions. After the movers packed everything, we proceeded in our Mercury Montego car to Victoria. The drive took five days, driving across the Prairies and through the mountains. We arrived in Victoria on Thanksgiving Day in November 1974. We had to stay in a hotel for two weeks as we waited for our furniture to arrive. We were excited to move into our new home in the Gordon Head area of Victoria.

I worked at the Pacific Forest Research Centre for over three years as Research Scientist and Project Leader. I enjoyed doing research and publishing in scientific journals and periodicals. I had the chance of attending meetings all over North

America and I made presentations about the results of my research work. I established a good working relationship with the U.S. Forest Service in Portland, Oregon and in Olympia, Washington, as well as with several of the universities in the Pacific Northwest. I also had a good working relationship with the B.C. Forest Service, Forest Productivity Committee, which was headed by Denis Glew (who was present at my demonstration in Sault Ste. Marie).

Dennis and I had a memorable trip to Oregon in the summer of 1976. The Forest Economists were holding a workshop in a resort town near Mount Hood. I took a Canadian Forest Service car and drove Denis to this meeting. Denis had a reputation for being fugal with his money. At times, he would even ask you for a coffee by saying, "I will let you buy me a coffee." With this in mind, when I traveled with Denis, I came across some interesting situations. After checking in at the resort hotel, we went to have dinner in a rather posh restaurant. I was a bit concerned that my government allowance might not cover the cost of the meal.

Denis, being a connoisseur of food and wine, ordered for both of us. When we had finished, Denis asked for the bill. I was relieved as I started to think that this expensive dinner would not provide a challenge for my relatively modest government allowance of $20 (CDN) with no provisions for entertaining clients and colleagues. When the waitress brought the bill, Denis turned to her and said, "My friend is treating me." and handed over the $65 (U.S.) bill to me. Since Denis was a valued associate, I felt obliged to pay for this lavish dinner, but, at the same time, I wanted to establish an even playing field for our future relationship.

Denis beamed when I accepted the bill. The next evening we went back to the same restaurant for dinner. This time I ordered T-bone steak for both of us and I asked Denis chose a wine that matched the top-of-the-line steak. When we had finished the meal, I asked for the bill and Denis was all smiles again. When the waitress came, I asked her to give the bill to my friend as it was his turn to treat me. Denis' facial expression indicated that he was unprepared for this surprise, but accepted to pay for the meal and looked at me with a guarded smile that I interpreted as "good on you". After that, Denis and I had a relationship where we took turns in treating each other without having to pay attention to whose turn it was.

I was publishing articles on computer simulation models[6], as well as contributing to a paper that was being presented by Denis and Terry at an International Conference in Norway[7]. In 1977, Denis Glew was promoted to be Forester in Charge of the

---

[6] Hegyi, F., 1975. *Growth Modeling in an Operational Planning Context*. Proc. Workshop on Canadian Forest Inventory Methods, Canadian Institute of Forestry. University of Toronto Press. pp 224-239.

[7] Glew, D.R., Hegyi, F. and Honer, T.G., 1976. *Data Base Requirements for Growth Models in the Computer Assisted Resource Planning System in British Columbia*. Proc. XVI IUFRO World Congress, Norway. pp 74-85.

Forest Inventory Division with the B.C. Forest Service. I continued to work with Denis, focusing on replacing manual methods with computer-driven processes. Around that time, metric conversion became a big challenge in Canada and it affected the forestry sector to a large extent. Denis was given the task of converting 7,320 forest cover maps from Imperial to Metric Scale.

Given the existing staff of draughtsman, it was estimated that the manual conversion would take about five years and would cost up to $5 million. Denis asked me and Frank Towler, Director of Information Systems Branch of the B.C. Forest Service, to research the possibility of doing the conversion with computers. Denis realized that this task would be a major assignment and created a new position for it: Forester in Charge of Research and Development. This position was advertised through the Public Service Commission. Denis suggested that I should apply for it, but made it clear that I had to win it on my own merit. In order to avoid any possible conflict of interest, he was not going to be involved in the selection process.

I went through the interview process and again, luck was on my side. I was offered the position by the Public Service Commission, in the summer of 1977, Denis Glew became my new boss. The office and computer facilities that came with the new job were considerably less than what I had enjoyed with the Canadian Forestry Service at the Pacific Forest Research Centre. My first assignment was to research the technology that was capable of converting forest cover maps into the Metric Scale. Frank Towler joined me in this research work. We set up the criteria for selection and then compared systems that were featured to have Computer-Assisted Mapping and Computer Graphics capabilities. We examined several companies with such capabilities and invited three to demonstrate how their software was capable of digitalizing a small sample of the B.C. forest cover maps.

M & S Computing had the best graphics capability so Denis Glew decided to visit the company in Huntsville, Alabama, in November 1977. Denis asked me to accompany him on this visit and to perform a scientific evaluation of the technology. John Mostert, a computer sales representative in Calgary, who was trying to represent M & S Computing in Canada, joined us for this trip.

M & S. was founded by Jim Medlock in 1969, a former IBM contractor who led the development of the guidance and control software for the Saturn V launch vehicle that sent astronauts to the moon. Their product was an Interactive Graphics Design System (IGDS) that was capable of digitalizing maps and then printing them at least to the quality that highly skilled draughtsman would produce. I spent a morning testing the capabilities of this exciting technology with the able assistance of John Hubbard, while Denis and VP Keith Schonrock discussed business arrangements, including staff training and maintenance issues. In the afternoons, we met President Jim Medlock and his wife, Nancy, who was the Controller of M & S Computing, to discuss purchasing options.

One afternoon, Keith took us on a tour of Redstone Arsenal. We had privileged access over the public and we were able to see the marvels of space research that was targeted to put a man on the moon. Dennis and I paused as we watched examples of scientific achievements, and commented that, "surely, there is technology to digitalize maps." Next we visited an office that left a life-long impression on me, the office of Dr. Wernher von Braun. It was a midsize office with real wood furniture (if I remember correctly, it was mahogany).

By the end of the week, Denis was satisfied that the 7,320 forest cover maps could be converted to the Metric Scale with the help of computer graphics. He informed Mr. Medlock that he would make a Treasury Board submission to get the funding, after which a tender would be issued. On Friday evening, we were invited to the house of Jim and Nancy Medlock for an afternoon cool down in the swimming pool, followed by dinner. While relaxing in the pool, we had a few gin and tonics and I was bragging a bit about how well I could cook.

Nancy asked me what is my specialty and I replied, "Hungarian goulash with Spaetzel." She asked if I would make that meal for supper.

Before I could respond, Denis said "Well of course, Frank is a good cook. I tasted that meal several times, so let's have it tonight."

Jim was delegated to get the ingredients while we continued with the spiritual enhancements in the pool. They had fillet mignon already at home, so Jim needed to get paprika, green pepper, tomatoes, onions, marjoram and caraway seed. The meal was a success, but Jim could not believe his eyes when I cut up the fillet mignon for goulash. He called it stew, which, to Hungarian ears, was not an acceptable description of the dish.

After returning to Canada, I was given the task of writing the Treasury Board submission to acquire a computer-assisted mapping system. Ted Evans was the Treasury Board Analyst who worked with me on the submission and when we submitted it to Dave Emerson, the Deputy Minister of Finance, it was turned down because the rationale had not been clearly articulated. I asked Ted to help me to resubmit it, but he told me that even he was not convinced that we were justified to spend $1.5 million on this acquisition. I made the proposition to Ted to come to the Branch for a day, observe how maps were made with the manual process, and if he was still not convinced, then we would accept the decision. Ted accepted this challenge and, at the end of the day, he agreed to help me to rewrite submission in a format that would convince the Deputy Minister to forward the request to Treasury Board. Within a period of three months, a budget of $1.5 million was approved and we proceeded with the acquisition of the system. In the meantime, M & S computing changed its name to Intergraph Corporation and John Mostert secured the distributorship of their products in Canada.

My job was to manage the system and train the staff of forty-five manual draughtsman in the new technology. This was especially challenging because their work environment changed from regular office hours to shift work and I had to negotiate this with a rather militant trade union. With a few exceptions, I managed to convince the staff that the introduction of a computer-assisted mapping system into mapmaking would provide them with new opportunities and reclassification to a higher level. In turn, they convinced the union to accept the reorganization proposal, including the shift work.

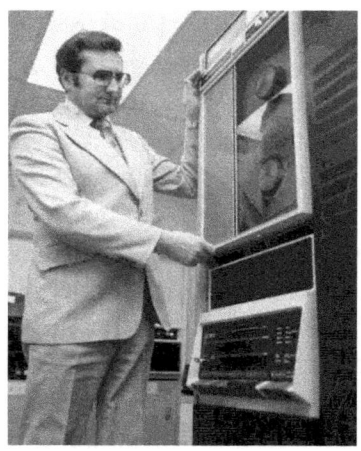

Picture 22. The graphics computer system.

Picture 23. The graphic and satellite image workstations.

In October 1978, Denis Glew decided to retire at the age of fifty-five. Since the Inventory Branch was going through a major reorganization, as well as changes in terms of modus operandi, of which I was the chief Architect, I was appointed Acting Director until the replacement for Denis could be selected. This was the trigger that created major problems for me. I was an outsider and a foreigner. In those days, foreigners never made it passed the position of manager in a very traditional organization. Not only that, but I was appointed Acting Director. I was turning the status quo upside down with computer-assisted draughting. The traditional draughting staff was up in arms saying that computers would never be able to replace the art of a draughtsman. They took me head on and were after blood.

In early December, we hosted a meeting of the Provincial and Federal Forest Inventory Chiefs, who were very interested in this new technology. It was the first one to be introduced in Canada into an operational environment. This meeting caught the attention of the press in Victoria, which put a pressure on the system to perform beyond its capabilities

In 1979, the B.C. Ministry of Forests undergoing some major changes. The new Ministry of Forests Act and the Forest Act introduced new concepts on how the over fifty million hectares of forest land should be managed. The computer-assisted mapping system that we had introduced was now recognized as being able to provide the tools needed for the implementation of changes. My position as Acting Director was still not accepted well by the "old guard". Fortunately for me, the B.C. Ministry of Forests named a new Deputy Minister, Mike Apsey, who was also an outsider. Mike and I were born in the same year and even had similar research background. I was very comfortable with the direction he set in place for the Forest Service. This made my job much easier.

In early 1979, I won the competition for the position of Director, Inventory Branch. This was not received well in an ultra-conservative Civil Service. Fortunately, the interview panel included people from the University of British Columbia and from the Public Service Commission. While traditionally, senior management was appointed from rank and file and especially from staff who had spent at least twenty years in the organization, the interview panel recognized that the Inventory Branch needed a leader who was familiar with the computer-assisted mapping technology. Since I was the most familiar one with the technology, I won the competition.

Some of the Hungarian forest engineers, those who had come from the University of Sopron in 1956 as a class and were now employed by the Ministry of Forests, were the most upset with my selection. I was an outsider, younger than them, came from the Federal Government, and was the first immigrant to reach the rank of a Director in the B.C. Forest Service. Now, I was their boss. I had a tough time winning the confidence of the old timers. I often heard them respond to the changes that I was introducing by saying, "We have done this way for twenty-five years, why change now?"

Besides the introduction of computer-assisted mapping technology, we changed the data collection from a subjective sampling method to a statistically based multiphase sampling system. The primary samples were obtained from 70 mm stereo pairs, a sub-sample of which was measured on the ground for validation and statistical adjustments. A further sub-sample was selected for periodic re-measurements in order to study growth and yield. In addition, I introduced satellite imagery to monitor the changes in forest cover due to harvesting and fire. The Canada Centre for Remote Sensing (CCRS) in Ottawa provided technical experts in the introduction of this pioneering technology which now completely frustrated many of the rank and file traditionalists. In particular, the Chief Research Scientist of CCRS, Dr. David Goodenough, took a personal interest in the application of remote sensing technology to map the forest resources of B.C. This provided additional credibility to the changes that I was proposing, and hence weakened the arguments of the traditional conservative opposition.

In order to introduce such new technologies operationally, I had to implement a major re-organization in the Forest Inventory Branch. I spent the 1979 Christmas holidays writing job descriptions that clearly specified scientific and technical knowledge requirements for all levels, including middle management. Members of the staff were then given three years to upgrade their qualifications to match the job descriptions of the positions that they currently held. I hired university professors to give workshops to the staff on the new sampling systems and satellite image analysis technology so that they could upgrade their knowledge within their own work environment. I had strong support for these changes from the Deputy Minister of Forests, Mike Apsey.

Except for three senior managers who decided to take early retirement rather than become involved with the new technology, the staff generally embraced the opportunities. One of these managers tried to block the changes by making a presentation to the Assistant Deputy Minister on emotional grounds. His argument was that he was a war veteran who was now being side-lined by the new immigrant who had come to Canada from a country that was aligned with Germany during the war. His argument was, "rejected with a stern warning that he might be in trouble with the Human Rights Commission over such views."

At the end of three years, we assessed the progress of staff in upgrading their skill sets and opened up some key positions for internal competition. Once all staff was assigned to the new positions, I asked the Public Service Commission to bring in a team to assess the classification of all of the jobs in the Branch. This was done over a six-month period and included 120 positions. Several of the jobs were re-classified into a higher level which involved promotions for the incumbents. At that point in time, the traditionalists who were putting up resistance to the introduction of new technology pulled back and gradually a new breed of managers emerged.

Visit to the Soviet Union

In the summer of 1980, a scientific delegation from the Soviet Union visited Canada. I was told by the Assistant Deputy Minister (also Chief Forester), Bill Young (who was my boss), that they expressed a strong interest in seeing a demonstration of the computer-assisted mapping system. When I looked at the list of visitors, I recognized the name of Dr. Moroz from a previous visit that he made to Sault Ste. Marie when I was working as a Computer Simulation Scientist. I said to Bill that I would be happy to give a demonstration for them, especially since I knew one of the visitors.

Our standard demo included a show-off of the resolution of the computer-assisted mapping system. Using the same design file, we created a graphic picture of the planet earth on which we could measure objects to 1 mm real world resolution. The design file included a map of North America, with zoom-in capabilities to the map of British Columbia, specifically the City of Victoria shown at street level detail. We even zeroed into the office building that we were in and the chair that the operator was sitting on. In the demo, we showed Planet Earth and measured its diameter to the nearest millimeter, zoomed into the various maps, and ended up measuring in the same design file the diameter of the chair that the operator was sitting on. Of course, this was verified by measuring the chair in front of the people watching the demo. Bill particularly liked this demo and suggested that we show it to the visitors. He suggested that we put a Canadian and a Soviet flag on the wall in the demo room. I said I would be pleased to hang the Canadian flag, "but please don't ask me to put up the red flag in my Branch. You know my background."

Bill's answer was: "How important is your job for you?"

I was cornered. That certainly did not leave me much choice. Bill had already arranged for the delivery of the flags from the Provincial Protocol Office. This was Friday morning and the demo was scheduled for Monday at 10 a.m. I asked Sue Chapman, who operated the computer graphics terminal for the demos, and two forest engineers of Ukrainian origin to come in on Saturday and help me with the preparations for the demo. I suggested that we label some components of the demo in Russian as a respect for my old friend Dr. Moroz.

On Saturday morning, when we met in the demo room, Steve Ilnytsky, one of the Ukrainians, saw the red flag and just about flipped out. I told him that it was the ADM's order. I had no choice in the matter. Since I had a good relationship with Dr. Moroz, I thought we should include some humor in the demo. I described the plan and it was strongly supported by the team. We set it up with labeling in Russian.

When the visitors arrived, I was a little nervous because they were accompanied by an official interpreter from the Department of Foreign Affairs and International Trade (DFAIT) from Ottawa as well as the B.C. Minister of Forests, Tom Waterland and Deputy Minister Mike Apsey. The leader of the delegation was Mr. Vorobjev and I understood that he was from the Ministry of Forests in Moscow. Mr. Vorobjev was a very tall man and had a face that never smiled. He even looked something like Brezhnev. Dr. Moroz greeted me warmly and noted that I had made a major career change from Research Scientist to High Tech Director.

We started the demo with Sue Chapman calling up the design file on the computer. I explained in English that we measured the polar diameter of the earth, which read as 12,756.32 km. The interpreter then translated what I said into Russian.

Once the interpreter finished translating, I switched over to Russian and said, "Now we zoom in on the map of the Soviet Union that we obtained from a Canadian reconnaissance satellite." The interpreter automatically translated this into English as everyone looked at me in shock, including the interpreter.

I continued in Russian, "We now zoom in to the city of Moskva." Sue zoomed into the street map of Moskva that we digitalized on Saturday, including labeling streets in Russian. Again, the interpreter translated it into English.

I switched back to English and asked Sue, "Please zoom in on that building. I believe it is the Luzhniki Stadium." Sue complied with my request and zoomed in to centre ice of the hockey arena.

I asked Sue, "Please zoom in further." Sue zoomed into the centre ice, showing both the Soviet and Canadian flags.

I said in Russian, "Oh, and look at the two flags at centre ice." The interpreter translated each sentence into English and, when I commented on the flags, my boss looked visibly upset (he had lost his sense of humor).

I continued anyway, asking Sue to zoom in further to the hockey puck that was between the two flags and to measure the diameter of the puck. Sue measured the diameter and showed it to be 77 mm.

I smiled and said, "There it is. The diameter of the puck should be 76.2 mm. That must be how the Soviet Union defeated team Canada in game 5 with a score of 5-4. They played with an illegal puck."

Before the interpreter could translate what I said, Dr. Moroz stood abruptly, smiled, came over to me and gave me a big hug. The Russians obviously appreciated my sense of humor, which is more than I can say for my boss who was absolutely furious.

We continued with the demo and the visitors were impressed with the capabilities of the computer-assisted mapping system. After the Soviet visitors left, I received a very mixed reaction to my sense of humor. Fortunately my Minister and Deputy Minister appreciated it, so I survived.

In 1982, it was the Russian's turn to host a Canadian scientific delegation in the Soviet Union. The Canadian Forestry Service (CFS) proposed Dr. Terry Honer, Dr. Mike Boner and a third person from Toronto who was of Ukrainian origin and spoke Russian. The Russians accepted Honer and Boner, but nominated me as the third person, giving the reason that they wanted an update on how we were progressing on the data management aspect of the computer-assisted mapping system. Initially, CFS objected to my selection on the grounds that I was not working for the Federal Government. An agreement was reached that the Federal Government would finance the costs associated with my visit.

The Foreign Affairs Department assured me that the Russians were aware of my background in 1956. The Russians guaranteed my safe travel in the Soviet Union. I was a bit nervous because, in Hungary, we were known as freedom fighters. In the eyes of the Russians, we were terrorists.

On the other hand, I was excited about visiting a country that I had studied extensively as a student. I purchased a Teach-Yourself-Russian tape that came with a booklet and started to refresh my memory with the language that I was able to converse in twenty-five years earlier. With the assistance of my staff, we prepared slides on the progress that we had made with the computer-assisted mapping system, each labeled in Russian.

On Saturday, June 19th 1982, I left Victoria at 11:30 a.m. and flew to Toronto via Vancouver. I met Terry Honer in Toronto and we departed at 8:55 p.m. on Air Canada to London. We arrived in London early in the morning where we met Mike Boner, who had flown in from Copenhagen where he had been visiting relatives. Around 11 a.m., the three of us boarded a Russian plane and, after we were airborne, they served what appeared to be vodka in a small glass.

I said to my colleagues, "Hey, we are getting vodka."

Journey to the Big World

Terry replied that he was not going to have any on a relatively empty stomach, especially since we would be traveling all night. I asked him to take it anyway because I was going to have it. Well, was I ever surprised when I drank the *vodka* and discovered that it was just plain water, not even cold?

Things changed, however, when we arrived in Moskva. We were treated like VIP's. As soon as we disembarked, we were escorted by high ranking police officers into the VIP lounge where Dr. Moroz and his colleagues were waiting for us. A very pleasant and attractive lady in her thirties came forward and greeted us in English. She introduced herself as Marina, the Official Interpreter. She offered to exchange U.S. dollars into Russian currency for us. Our hosts toasted us with vodka several times and there was lots of salami and caviar on bread.

After about an hour of this warm reception, we were taken by car to our hotel, which ironically was Hotel Budapest. We were then left alone for the night. Even Marina the Interpreter went home. This was about 6 p.m. on Sunday. We had not eaten any supper as of yet. After we checked into our rooms and unpacked, we went down to the dining room at around 8 p.m.

I was the interpreter for the group, which was challenging, to say the least. We had to wait twenty minutes to be seated. We noticed that three ladies, who had been waiting before us, were seated at a table for six. We were then seated at that same table. The ladies started to talk. They knew a few words in English, the rest I had to fill in. We ordered cold cuts with bread and salad and Georgian red wine. There was an excellent band playing music and the ladies asked us to dance.

We thought it was nice Russian hospitality, until after the second dance. I was called out of the dining room by the head waiter. A petit lady greeted me in broken English, "What are your intentions?"

I replied that we were just having dinner and being polite.

She replied, "You were dancing with my girls. What are your intentions?"

I realized that it had been a set up. I returned to the table. We ordered a bottle of Hungarian champagne for the ladies, paid our bills and went to our rooms. We were convinced that they were planted there by KGB. Next morning when Marina arrived to pick us up, we asked her to move us into a room that had three beds. She was not too happy about this request, but agreed. From then on, we always shared a room in order to avoid being in a compromising situation, including the possibility of being framed.

On same morning, Marina came with two government cars to pick us up. We were taken to meet Dr. Moroz, the Director of Lezprojekt, who was responsible for the Forest Inventory and Planning program of all of the Soviet Union. Dr. Moroz had a large office with old-fashioned furniture. We were served soda water, vodka and coffee. He greeted us warmly and mentioned that he enjoyed visiting Canada and hoped that we would enjoy our visit to the Soviet Union.

Dr. Moroz and his staff gave us a good overview of their program, which consisted of ground samples and manual preparation of forest cover maps. The Soviets used very little remote sensing technology and had not implemented computer-assisted mapping technology into their operations. Hence, they had a strong interest in the technology that we were pioneering in British Columbia.

We spent Monday morning with Dr. Moroz and, in the afternoon, we visited the different departments within Lezprojekt. In the evening, Dr. Moroz hosted a dinner with lots of vodka and wine. On Tuesday, Marina took us to the Kremlin. We visited the tomb of Lenin and the Russian Orthodox Church that Marina called "a museum". We also visited the University of Moskva and had a tour of the city by car. Actually, we traveled in three cars, Marina was in the one with Terry and Mike, I was in another with one of Dr. Moroz's staff and a security officer and the third car carried plain cloths police officers (probably KGB).

In the evening, we were taken to see a circus performance, which was very entertaining. On Wednesday, we visited the Forest Research Institute at Pushkino near Moskva, as well as the town of Zagorsk which was about seventy kilometers from Moskva. Zagorsk is the home of the Moscow Theological Academy and Troitse Sergieva Lavra (monastery), founded in the fourteenth century by Sergei Kadonezhski. For centuries, it had been the largest religious and cultural centre of Russia. It was like going back in time a few hundred years. The elderly women who worked there wore black dresses. Each time an Orthodox priest came by, they gave the sign of the cross and bent in front of the priest several times. Our interpreter, Marina, commented that Zagorsk was supported by the Soviet Regime as part of the religious freedom, but only a few of the elderly people participated in the religion.

Picture 24. Mr. Moroz (dark suit) explaining the Soviet system to the Canadian delegation.

Picture 25. Marina, the interpreter, on a visit to the museum in Petersburg.

On Thursday June 24th, we returned to Lezprojekt where I gave a slide presentation in Russian to Dr. Moroz and his staff, with a bit of help from Marina. They were very impressed with our technology of computer-assisted mapping and satellite image analysis. One of the scientists said that they were also working with such a technology, but it was at another location and we wouldn't have time to visit that building. We concluded that the work must be classified and that the building must be located within a military compound.

We went for lunch with Dr. Moroz around 2 p.m. Lunch started with lots of vodka, caviar, salami, black bread, followed by borsch and fried chicken. I was very surprised that the borsch was made with white beets, unlike the one my mother-in-law makes which was with red beets (the Ukrainian type). I mentioned this to Dr. Moroz and he was very impressed with my knowledge of the Ukrainian cuisine (he was born in Kiev).

On Thursday evening, we were hosted by the Canadian embassy for a reception and Dr. Moroz and his staff was also invited. This was very much appreciated by our hosts. There were lots of toasts made to international friendship and cooperation. I was enjoyed the evening very much and it took my mind back to 1956. Here we were colleagues, offering each other friendship and mutual respect. Yet, just over twenty-five years ago, the politics made us hate each other and, in the eyes of the Russians, I had been labeled a teenage terrorist.

On Friday, Marina took us on another tour around Moskva, including a ride on the subway, which was very clean and running efficiently. That evening we checked out of the hotel and were taken to the railway station. The train left at midnight for Leningrad (now St. Petersburg), our next stop. It was a fascinating trip. Marina could get only one cabin which had two beds and that was given to Terry and Mike. I went with Marina into another cabin that had four beds. She explained that another two persons could potentially join us at any of the stations and she felt that I would be able to adjust to it better since I could speak some Russian, as well as had a better background in Russian customs than did Terry and Mike.

When daylight broke, we could see the countryside as we traveled through small villages. We saw the typical country houses with shingle roofs and brick walls, with chickens in the back and large vegetable gardens. It was very similar to the villages in Hungary and brought to life the descriptions of the countryside in Leo Tolstoy's novels. We arrived in Leningrad on Saturday morning and were received by some of the staff who worked in the regional office of Lezprojekt. They took us to our hotel and we were left there to rest until about 2 p.m.

Mr. Andropov (not the KGB head), Director of the Regional Lezprojekt office, was our host in Leningrad. He was also a famous hockey referee (NHL status) and appeared to have been well connected. In the evening, he took us to a nice restaurant for a meal, then to really classy theatre where we had excellent seats in the third row. On Sunday morning, he showed us their offices, which were similar to those we had toured in Moskva. Right after lunch, he took us to the Hermitage Museum which was an experience of a lifetime. When we arrived at the museum, the lineup to get in was very long. Mr. Andropov took us in through a side door (after showing a special ID card to the security officer). We spent several hours walking around seeing all of the incredible works of art. Unfortunately, we were not allowed to take any pictures inside.

On Monday morning, I gave a slide presentation to the staff at the regional office, again in Russian with the help of Marina. The presentation was followed by good discussions on the different approaches to mapping forests. Mr. Andropov and I had a long talk about hockey when he found out that I was involved with the Minor Hockey Administration in Canada.

On Monday afternoon, we traveled by plane (Aeroflot) to Kiev, Ukraine. We were hosted there again by the staff of the regional Lezprojekt office. I found the Ukrainian culture and cuisine very interesting. My mother-in-law had been only six-months-old when her parents came with her to Canada, but she grew up in Saskatchewan the old country way. She still practiced the old ways, whereas the people in the Ukraine had changed considerably in the past fifty years. The food we ate in Kiev was a little different than what my mother-in-law called typical Ukrainian food.

On Tuesday June 29th, we visited the Lezprojekt office and they gave us a good overview of the Ukrainian program, focusing a lot on research in tree growth projections. In the evening, we were honoured by a nice dinner, again, with lots of vodka. I was getting quite daring with my knowledge of the Russian language and offered them a toast which I thought was typically Ukrainian, having learnt it from my mother-in-law. Each time we were at her place for dinner, we always toasted with, "daj borzse". When I offered this toast, they had a good chuckle because under Communism they couldn't toast with, "God give".

Instead, they used, "Za vashe zdorov'e", which means, "to your health". When I recited a few verses of the world's most romantic love letter in Russian, were they ever surprised? Even Marina couldn't believe that I remembered from High School *Tatyana's letter to Onegin.*

This was followed with more vodka, the strength of which was still with us the next morning. I had a good supply of Rolaids on hand, which I shared with our Ukrainian hosts. It was a gesture that was well received.

On Wednesday, June 30th, we visited the Botanical Gardens in Kiev, which showcased many different tree species. On July 1st, we ate breakfast in the hotel with our hosts then we were transported to the airport to fly back to Moskva. I was supposed to fly to Budapest in the evening, but was told that we were all summoned to see somebody in Moskva first thing in the morning. Marina asked for our passports so that she could process our exit papers. We were then left in the hotel and I couldn't help but wonder, *what was the reason for changing my flight from Thursday evening to Friday morning*?

Marina joined us for breakfast on Friday morning. After breakfast, I checked out of the hotel, put my luggage in one of the cars, and we left to visit this mysterious person. When we arrived at our destination, it was obviously a government building, and the sign said: Ministry of Forests, All Union States. Marina escorted us into a posh office that had a sign on the door: "Minister". We sat down and in came Dr. Moroz with Mr. Vorobjev, who was the Minister of Forest for All Union States. At that moment, I thought I'd die. After all, in Victoria, I had played

Journey to the Big World

that joke about the Canadian Spy Satellite on a Communist Cabinet Minister.

Mr. Vorobjev greeted us with a handshake. He was still not smiling as he sat down. He informed me that he had been impressed with what I had demonstrated in Victoria. He asked what I thought of Soviet technology in comparison. I replied that I was very impressed with what I saw. I noted that we obviously had different approaches, although we were traveling on parallel courses. I said that I found the trip to be intellectually stimulating.

Mr. Vorobjev turned to Dr. Moroz and commented, "Our friend has become a diplomat since our last meeting." He stood up, walked towards me and said, "Mr. Hegyi, I understand that you are not going back to Canada directly, but going to visit your mother, Sarolta, and father, Ferenc, in the village of Nyögér where you were a youth leader in the counter revolution in 1956."

At that point, I almost visualized Siberia as my next destination. I just froze when he knew the first name of my parents and the details of 1956. Terry and Mike told me afterward that I went so white in the face that they thought that I was about to pass out. Mr. Vorobjev continued, offering a handshake, "I just want to wish you personally a nice visit with your parents. We are very proud of what you accomplished away from home. We all want to forget 1956."

I was visibly relieved when Mr. Vorobjev shook my hand and gave me a big smile. He asked if I was scared of what was going to happen. I replied, "That is an understatement, sir."

Mr. Vorobjev shook hands with Dr. Moroz and said to him, "We got him real good for the spy satellite joke." That was when I realized that Mr. Vorobjev could smile.

Marina took me to the airport to catch my flight to Budapest. After I checked in my luggage, I said goodbye to Marina, thanked her for looking after us so well, then proceeded to the secure passport control area. Fortunately, Marina was still waiting outside to make sure that I passed through without any problem. The officer in border guard uniform was asking me where was the stamped paper that showed how much Russian currency I purchased when I arrived in Moskva. I did not have that paper because Marina had done the exchange for us and had forgotten to give it to me. The officer refused to stamp my passport to let me out of the country. He waved to his superior to come over to see what they wanted to do with me. At that point, Marina joined us and tried to explain what had happened and that I was on an official visit to the Soviet Union from Canada. She explained that she had exchanged the money and the paper must be in her office.

The officer was insistent, "No, he cannot leave the country without that paper."

Marina opened her purse and pulled out her badge. She showed it to the officer and ordered him, "Stamp the passport now comrade."

He saluted her with, "Yes, Comrade Major."

That was when I realized that our escort and interpreter, this charming lady with whom we had nice conversations, was in fact a Major in the KGB. Marina saw the surprised look on my face. She gave me a hug and whispered in my ear, "Have a nice trip. You are fine. Nothing will happen to you."

I was flying with Malev, the Hungarian airline to Budapest. It was nice that I understood the language. I enjoyed the Hungarian food and wine, but couldn't help wondering if I said anything to Marina that would haunt me while I was visiting another Communist country. Fortunately, nothing happened. I stayed in Hungary for two weeks and went back to Victoria on July 17th.

The day after my return to Victoria, I had two plain cloths RCMP officers visit me in my office. I briefed them on our encounters and the response was, "You made the right decision."

International Adventures

The introduction of computer-assisted mapping and Geographic Information Systems (GIS) into operational applications in natural resource management was considered, at the time, to be state-of-the-art technology with a futuristic context. Our program in British Columbia was leading this futuristic thrust and, as a result, I was invited to talk about it at several international conferences and workshops. I tried to illustrate each presentation with slides that demonstrated how the system was applied, what the outputs looked like and delivered the key messages in terms of humorous anecdotes. I was also invited to serve on advisory committees to Canadian government agencies. This opportunity opened new doors on the international circuit.

For ten years, I had served on the Canadian Advisory Committee on Remote Sensing (CACRS), which was charged with providing advice to the Canada Centre for Remote Sensing on the applications of space products to Natural Resource Management. For two years I also chaired a subcommittee of CACRS that involved provincial and territorial government agencies (IPTASC: Inter Provincial and Territorial Advisory Sub-Committee). In that capacity, I was asked to make a presentation to the Inter Agency Committee on Space (consisting of federal Deputy Ministers) in support of lunching RADARSAT I for mapping Canada's resources. Dr. Ed Shaw, who was the Chief Scientist working on the design of RADARSAT I, assisted me in this presentation and our efforts were well received by the Deputy Ministers.

For ten years, I had also served on the Canadian Forest Inventory Committee (CFIC) that was trying to integrate data from the provincial forest inventory systems into a national data base. This was particularly challenging because the provincial agencies designed their systems based on standards that were aligned to the provincial forest resource management mandates. Hence, the integration of data that was collected in terms of incompatible standards was a challenging task and demanded some major compromises and flexibilities.

The most interesting advisory committee that I was asked to serve on was the Futuristic Advisory Committee that was chaired by Professor Angus Hamilton, Chairman, and Surveying Engineering at the University of New Brunswick. We reported to the Associate Deputy Minister of Energy, Mines and Mineral Resources of the Canadian Government. We were charged with looking into the future in terms of technology that would become available to map Canada's natural resources. Our imagination had no limits and the resulting predictions have proven to be on target, as has been verified by the technology development during the past twenty or more years.

Concerning the international scene, I received invitations to make presentations at some interesting conferences. For example, in November 1985, I was invited to give a Keynote Address in Ottawa at an Inter-Regional Seminar on the Role of Surveying, Mapping and Charting in Country Development Programming, sponsored by the United Nations, CIDA and

Canada Department of Energy, Mines and Resources. My talk was scheduled for 9 a.m. on Tuesday, November 5th. On Monday afternoon, I attended some workshops on GIS. One was given by a vendor (not Intergraph), which lasted for an hour. The other one was given by a consultant, which lasted for another two hours. I thought that both workshops were promoting the same vendor rather than helping users to choose a GIS that was most appropriate for their application.

As a result of my impressions, my opening address over 800 attendees the following started, "Last night I had a dream." Laughter rippled through the audience. Everyone believed that I was referring to Dr. Martin Luther King. Little did they know that on August 28, 1963, I had been in the Amazon rainforest and, consequently, I was unfamiliar about this particular speech of Dr. King?

I continued, "I dreamed that Treasury Boards across Canada would come to realize the importance of this new technology called computer-assisted mapping and Geographic Information Systems (GIS) and urge people who were involved in surveys and mapping to purchase the necessary hardware and software."

This brought even more laughter because the toughest task that we were all facing at the time was to convince Provincial and Federal Treasury Boards to release money for the modernization of surveying and mapping.

I continued with my presentation, hoping to make an impact based on the comments made by the previous day's presenters. "Then next I was facing the firing squad. There were

Journey to the Big World

three of us: the GIS vendor, the consultant and I, the user of GIS. We were all given a wish before being shot. The GIS vendor said, "Let me give an hour lecture that my GIS is the best." The GIS consultant said, "Let me give a two hour lecture on how to select a GIS so that you will select the one my friend here sells." I then said. "Just shoot me first."

I was given a standing ovation. The people who I referred to left the room and have not spoken to me since.

Picture 26. A certificate for my effort.

Because of the comments I made at the Ottawa conference, I was asked to address another meeting in Winnipeg the following year, with a focus on what to look for in selecting a

GIS vendor. I tried to illustrate my talk by comparing it to buying a shirt. I was wearing a pin-striped suit, white shirt and red tie. I told the audience that buying a GIS is like buying a shirt. In both cases, one had to be careful not to rely completely on what the sales person told you, but to examine the product in terms of its intended use. Next I showed the cuffs on my shirt and said, "The salesman told me that they would never wear out, and after five years, they would look like new." I pointed to the collar of the shirt and said, "The salesman also said that the collar will never wear out." I bought the shirt because the salesman assured me that I only needed to concern myself with those two things when buying a shirt. I turned around, took off my jacket and showed the back of the shirt, which was torn to shreds. Conclusion: check out all aspects when buying either a shirt or a GIS.

In the summer of 1985, I received a telephone call from Dr. Abe Abiodun, who worked in the Office of Outer Space Affairs of the United Nations in Vienna, Austria. Dr. Abiodun was organizing a historic workshop in Beijing, China, on the Peaceful Uses of Outer Space products. He invited me to give a presentation on how the B.C. Government was using satellite imagery in the management of its natural resources. I accepted the invitation and obtained a visa from the Chinese Embassy in Vancouver on October 16, 1985, just in time to start my journey on October 22nd. My flight was through Narita, Japan, where I stayed overnight on October 23rd and flew to Beijing on the next day. After checking in at the hotel, I registered for the workshop and asked one of the interpreters if she would help me to learn a few words in Mandarin. She was pleased to oblige and we spent a couple of hours in this venture. My presentation was in the morning of Friday, October 25th.

Unfortunately, I forgot to buy mineral water on Thursday afternoon when I arrived in the hotel, so on Friday morning I had to use scotch to wash my teeth. I was in relatively good spirits when I started my presentation, which, of course, was illustrated with slides. I opened my talk with greetings to the audience in Mandarin, thanking the Chinese organizers for their outstanding hospitality, and expressing how honored I was for the opportunity to participate in this historic meeting. When I finished these sentences in Mandarin, the Chinese attendees in the audience gave me a standing ovation. The workshop ended on Saturday, and, on Sunday October 27th, I again asked the interpreter who helped me to learn some Mandarin, where could I rent a car with a driver for a few hours so that I could look around Beijing. Within half an hour, a driver appeared who spoke some English and said that he had a government car for the day. He offered to take me around. When I asked how much it would cost me, he said that it was a courtesy car supplied by the Organizing Committee to show their appreciation for the efforts I made in learning a little bit of Mandarin. Apparently my attempt at speaking Mandarin had been interpreted as a sign of respect towards the Chinese people.

The first stop was Tiananmen Square where I attracted a lot of attention while I took pictures. We then drove out to see the Great Wall, which was especially interesting. I marveled at the amount of work that most have gone into building the wall over 2000 years ago.

Picture 27. Me on the Great Wall of China.

When we returned to the hotel, I thanked my hosts for their kind hospitality. I joined some of the fellow delegates for dinner. I was looking for the typical Chinese cuisine that I was used to in Canada, just to realize that the Canadian version is mainly Cantonese and that was not available in Beijing at the time. On October 28th, I left Beijing with some fond memories and a greater appreciation of the history of people on this earth.

Journey to the Big World

In 1988, I had another opportunity to visit China on a project funded by the Canadian International Development Agency (CIDA). The project was started in 1984 and was called an Integrated Intensive Forest Management (IIFM) project. Canadian contribution was over $10 million and the delivery of Canada's contribution was the responsibility of CIDA. After a competitive selection process involving many Canadian firms, CIDA engaged the services of a consortium composed of T.M. Thomson and Associates and Reid, Collins and Associates to act as the Canadian executing agency responsible for the delivery of Canada's contribution. I was seconded by the B.C. Government to evaluate how the forest inventory components were being implemented. We first flew to Beijing, stayed overnight and proceeded to Harbin the next day. We spent a few days in Harbin in meetings with Chinese officials. The second night, the Canadian delegation, consisting of eight persons, including the Under-Secretary from the Canadian Embassy, was hosted for a banquet by the Vice-Governor of Harbin. When we opened the menu, it spelled out who footed the bill: "the Ministry of Social Intercourse". Well, sometimes translations can take on a different meaning.

The following day we traveled by train to the project site, which was in Langxiang, Heilongjiang Province, Northern China. We stayed in a government guest house where the hospitality was outstanding. The meetings were well organized and we were taken on a tour of the town to see the market and other attractions. I was learning a little bit of Mandarin again, as well as enjoying some real Chinese cooking. One thing led to another, I was invited to cook Hungarian goulash for the Canadians and our hosts. We went to the market to buy pork (beef was not available) and other ingredients (at least most of what I needed). I cooked rice as a side dish to the goulash and we all learned to eat it with chop sticks. I learned that sharing each other's' culture was an effective way of communicating mutual respect for one other, even though we came from totally different backgrounds.

One evening, as we were hosted for dinner, one of the interpreters took sick and I ended up sitting next to a Chinese forest engineer who did not speak any English. Since Langxiang was not too far from the Russian border, I took a chance to find out if he spoke Russian. When I asked him, he replied in Russian. We were able to maintain a courteous conversation. Now that we were talking, and since he was from China, he immediately assumed the role of being my host. The drinks that were served included wine and Chinese white liquor called maotai.

My host lifted his glass and said. "Ganbei" ("bottoms up"). I have been known to be able to hold my liquor, but we reached double digits with ganbei, featuring mainly the firewater called maotai. At the end of the banquet, my host needed assistance in leaving the room as he found his legs were like rubber. I looked across the table at the Canadian Undersecretary, Mr. Henderson, and his wife who were very amused at what had happened. They told me that it was my fault that he was drunk. I had violated a local custom. They had tried to tip me off, but I was not getting it. The truth was that I have a habit of holding my glass during socializing. According to the local custom, as soon as I touched the glass again after putting it down, the people serving were obliged to fill it up again and my host was obliged, in turn, to say, "Bottoms up."

After spending two weeks in Langxiang, I traveled to Bangkok, Thailand, where I presented an invited paper on Key Factors in an Operational GIS for Land Use Planning, at a Workshop organized by the United Nations, ESCAP/UNDP program.

In early 1988, Dr. Leo Sayn-Wittgenstein, Director General of the Canada Centre for Remote Sensing, was visiting the Inventory Branch in Victoria to see how we were progressing with the integration of remote sensing and GIS technologies. After the meeting, I invited Leo for dinner at our home where I offered to cook Hungarian goulash. After dinner, we talked about international activities and he asked me if I would allow my name to be proposed for the Presidency of Commission VII, International Society of Photogrammetry and Remote Sensing (ISPRS). By this time, we had paid our respect to a bottle of Egri Bikavèr (Hungarian wine which is also called Bull's Blood) and, since I was not familiar with the activities of ISPRS, I said that it was fine with me. I considered this gesture by Leo to be simply a compliment and expected it not to go any further.

I was surprised a month later to be contacted by the Canadian Institute of Surveying and Mapping (CISM), who was the official member of ISPRS on behalf of Canada, asking me to confirm that I would be attending the XVI International Congress of ISPRS that was being held in Kyoto, Japan. I said that I was not planning on it. I didn't even know anything about it. I was told that this was very problematic since Canada submitted my name for Commission VII President. I remembered the dinner meeting with Leo and the indulgence in Egri Bikavèr, and backpedaled fast by saying that I would be willing to honor the commitment I had made with Leo. I asked them to please send me details of the congress because I needed to get the Minister's approval for international travel of this nature. They sent the detail by mail and, when we saw that this was an honor for B.C., I was granted permission to attend, with expenses paid by the B.C. Government.

When I arrived in Kyoto on July 3rd, 1988, I was called to a meeting organized by Dr. Robin Steeves, President of CISM, which was also attended by Hugh O'Donnell, Assistant Deputy Minister with the Federal Department of Energy, Mines and Resources (EMR) responsible for the National Surveys, Mapping and Remote Sensing Programs. Hugh had indicated that EMR would provide some financial support towards this activity because visibility in this area was important for Canada as Canadian industry would have major opportunities in the international arena, especially as GIS projects came up for bids. I was told that we were facing heavy competition for this position from the Soviet Union and Britain.

We met with Canadians who were attending the Congress and Dr. Pam Sallaway volunteered to be campaign chairperson with the assistance of Dr. Mosaad Allam. Traditionally, Technical Commission presidents were either from Universities or Research Institutes who focused on developing new techniques in Photogrammetry. The delegation from Britain approached Hugh and I and suggested that we withdraw in order to avoid embarrassment. They had a candidate who was a famous professor from the University of London and they expected him to win, although the Soviet Union also had a well-known scientist from the Space Agency. This made the Canadian team even more enthused to work harder on the campaign. Hugh O'Donnell, who spoke French perfectly, had the ear of the French delegation; Pam Sallaway was well respected by the GIS community and women scientists; Mosaad Allam (originally from Egypt) campaigned effectively among delegates who spoke Arabic; and I had good connections with the delegates from China, Thailand and countries who were under Soviet domination. I found it exciting to go for it when the chances of success for us were considered to be limited by the international community. This was another opportunity to dare to take the next step.

I gave a slide presentation on our work with the integration of GIS and Remote Sensing and suggested that there was a major opportunity for ISPRS to expand from the academic environment into operations where their science was very much needed, but in the terminology that users could understand.

The voting started. The candidate from Britain had the lowest votes and had to drop out. The next round, Canada defeated the Soviet Union, and I was elected President of Commission VII with a focus on GIS and Remote Sensing Applications.

The Executive and Technical Commission Presidents of ISPRS met once a year in different countries. In 1989, we met in Zurich, Switzerland. In 1990, I hosted the meeting in Victoria. The 2001 meeting was held in Glasgow, Scotland, and, in 2002, we met in Washington D.C. on the occasion of the XVII International Congress. Each Technical Commission President was required to organize a mid-term Symposium. I organized the Commission

Journey to the Big World

VII Symposium in Victoria, B.C., which was held September 17 to 21, 1990. Over 240 papers from twenty-three countries had been reviewed by the Scientific Committee and a total of 192 were accommodated in four concurrent sessions.

There were two plenary sessions, one at the start of the conference on Tuesday morning and the other at its conclusion on Friday. There were twelve workshops covering the following topics: Geographic Information Systems (GIS) Concepts; GIS Applications for Management; GIS Applications for Operators; Satellite Image Analysis (SIA) Concepts; SIA Applications for Operators; Photogrammetry and Photo-interpretation Concepts; Aerial Photo Interpretation; Radar Concepts and Applications; Expert Systems and Artificial Intelligence; Remote Sensing for Teachers and Educators; and Environmental Site Assessment and Monitoring. Over 400 international delegated participated in the Symposium.

My term as President of ISPRS Commission VII was coming to an end during the 1992 congress that was held in Washington, D.C. Each Commission President was charged with organizing workshops on topics that fell under their area of scientific responsibility. I organized twenty-three different workshops, which were held during the period August 3 to 14, 1992. Each workshop had a focus on futuristic technology in the area of Photogrammetry and Remote Sensing. Attendance exceeded all expectations.

Volunteering to Repay Society

Now that I was settled in Canada, I believed it was time to repay my debt to society. The helping hand offered to me by so many people made it possible for me to get this far in life. My first volunteer work was with the Sault Pee Wee Minor Hockey Association. I worked with them as Public Relations Director, writing articles in the newspaper and appearing on television to publicize the good work of the Association, as well as getting businesses to sponsor the various hockey teams. I also helped out managing a Pee Wee B team.

After recovering from my bout with crippling arthritis in 1971, I learned to walk without a cane. Then I decided to learn to skate. I had never had the opportunity skate while growing up in Hungary. I became the coach of the Pee Wee B team that was in last place the previous year. Because they were under-performers, the Association couldn't find a coach for them, so I volunteered. For the practices, I would bring in a top midget hockey player to teach them the skills that they needed. My job was to motivate the players, to give them confidence and to manage the lines during the games.

Before each game, I asked the players, "Who is the best team?"

They answered, "We are."

I told them, "I didn't hear you."

With greater gusto, they would say it again, "We are."

We repeated this a few times before going out to play all fired up. My third line had the same ice time as the other two, and never shouted at any player (which was different from many of the other coaches). I complimented the good plays and gave encouragement to a player when he ended up in the net instead of the puck, telling him, "Better luck next time. Keep up the good work."

Our team progressed from last place to win both the League and the Playoff Championships in the spring of 1972. This team was sponsored by the Lakeshore Kiwanis Club and the one we defeated was sponsored by ACT. I was buying pop for the player's right after winning the playoff championship and the ACT coach, Con Lauber, came over to congratulate me as he was helping the ACT representative buy the drinks for his team.

I took the drinks to the dressing room, returning to talk to Con. I said, "You have a good sponsor. They buy pop for the players even when they lose. We won the championship and I haven't seen anybody from the Kiwanis Club. You would think that somebody would at least come out to watch the final game."

Con smiled and explained, "Kiwanis is going to give the players and parents a banquet. They are very proud of how the team played and how you coached them."

I said, "How do you know that?"

He answered, "Because I am the President of the Lakeshore Kiwanis Club." Con went on to tell me that he would like to invite me to join the club. After opening my big mouth, how could I refuse?

Journey to the Big World

In 1972, I became a member of the Kiwanis Club of Lakeshore in Sault Ste. Marie. During the 1972-73 hockey season, I coached again the hockey club that was sponsored by Kiwanis. My son, Michael, decided to join our team. He performed well enough to win the vote of his teammates to become the Captain of the team. We had a fun-filled season and won again both the League and the Playoff Championships. It was especially rewarding for me to be able to work with Michael on the ice as I was still learning to skate. Con was there for the final game and teased me that, as a Kiwanian, I was now obliged to buy the pop for the players without complaining.

Picture 28. I coached the Kiwanis team to championship. My son Michael was the team captain.

In 1973, I was asked to work with the Novice Tournament Team as manager, with Walter Dubas as coach. I sure learned a lot about hockey from Walter, who coached before the Sault Greyhounds, a Major Junior team in the OHL. Our star player was Ronnie Francis. I gave him the No. 10 sweater. He retained that number in the NHL where he was captain of two teams.

Picture 29. I managed the Novice tournament team. The team captain was Ronnie Francis, who became an NHL captain

In 1973 I also chaired the conservation committee for Kiwanis. Our big project was planting trees in new subdivisions in Sault Ste. Marie. First, we canvassed the houses and asked the owners if they would like a tree planted by Kiwanis in the front yard. If they said yes, then we asked them to dig a hole to our specs a few days before Arbor Day. Kiwanis then purchased the trees, which were about five to six feet high. On Arbor Day, Kiwanis members came out in full force to do the delivery and the planting. Chairing an active committee and coaching a hockey team earned me a very prestigious award at the end of 1973: *Kiwanian of the Year.*

I continued the volunteer work with Kiwanis when we moved to Victoria in 1974 by joining the Kiwanis club of Victoria. In the first year, I was asked to chair the Youth Services Committee, which previously had not been very active. One of the members of this committee was Inspector Dick Ward of the Victoria Police Department. The committee had eight other members, all very keen on coming up with a project. Dick brought Constable Ken Dibden to one of our meetings. Ken was a motorcycle cop and made a presentation to our committee promoting the idea of working with youth who had been referred to them by the court as having the potential for getting out of trouble. Ken suggested that if Kiwanis would buy ten motorbikes, seventy-five cc dirt bikes, he and some of his fellow officers would take them out on Saturdays and teach them how to ride. The catch was that they could only remain in the club if they kept out of trouble and would attend school regularly.

We worked out a budget and documented how the program would work, including its benefits to the community. I made a presentation to the Board of Directors of the Kiwanis Club. The Board approved the budget and we had a good project that was growing a little bit each year. We even managed to purchase a van to transport the bikes. On the sides of the van was written, "Kiwanis Wheels project sponsored by the Victoria Police and the Kiwanis Club of Victoria."

Since this project was very successful, received good publicity for Kiwanis in the newspapers and on television, I was awarded again the honor, *Kiwanian of the Year* in 1976.

In 1975, the Oak Bay Minor Hockey Association was created in Victoria. Larry LaRochelle was its first president and I was Director of Public Relations. The following year (1976), I was elected president and my main focus was to create a better relationship between the eleven minor hockey associations on south Vancouver Island.

Each minor hockey association had a tournament team in the pee wee, bantam, midget and junior B category that played in a loosely organized league. My efforts were well received and we created the South Vancouver Island Minor Hockey Association (SVIMHA). In June 1977, I was elected as its charter president.

Even before the hockey season would could begin, I was called to a meeting with Ken King, Manager of the Harbor Towers Hotel, to discuss the possibility of Victoria hosting an old-timers" hockey tournament. I asked some of the executives of SVIMHA to attend this meeting with me and to see if we, as an association, were interested in participating. The meeting was held on Friday, August 19, 1977. Jim Orr, Technical Director and Referee in Chief of the Canadian Oldtimers' Hockey Association (COHA) made a presentation about the organization. COHA was founded in October of 1974 by John F. Gouett in Peterborough, Ontario. The First National Oldtimers' Hockey Tournament was held in Peterborough, Ontario, in February 1975. The major success of the First National Oldtimers' Hockey Tournament that brought fifty-six teams and over 1000 players together was the foundation that John utilized for his development of the COHA as a national sports' association. COHA was recognized by the Government of Canada (Recreation Canada) to provide programs and services for its membership across Canada and internationally.

Jim told us that the first annual Pacific Cup Tournament was held on the mainland in January 1977. It was fairly successful, although he thought that the City of Victoria would be a more suitable place to hold annual tournaments. Victoria had a better climate in January and there were ten hockey rings within half an hour of travel from city hotels. Ken King was also a member of the Victoria Tourism Bureau and he could see right away the benefits of fifty oldtimers hockey teams arriving in Victoria during tourism's off season (i.e., January).

Jim Orr described the resources needed to run a tournament of about fifty teams. He said that besides the arenas, there needed to be a Host Committee consisting of about twenty chairs coordinating over 200 volunteers. By this time, I had built up a reputation in minor hockey that I was able to get volunteers for hockey activities, and the executive members of SVIMHA who were present at the meeting volunteered me as chairman of the Host Committee. Jim Orr felt comfortable about working with us to host the tournament.

The next day, Saturday August 20th, I called a meeting of the SVIMHA Executive and we started to recruit Host Committee members. By Tuesday, August 23rd, we had recruited over 200 volunteers. After that, some of the volunteers joked, "If Frank

Journey to the Big World

Hegyi tells you "let me buy you a beer", run because it will be the most expensive drink you will ever have."

A special guest of the tournament was the legendary hockey player, Fred (Cyclone) Taylor, who dropped the puck and then was presented a gift by Victoria's Mayor, Michael Young.

The tournament had fifty-two teams participating, playing a total of ninety-six games in five arenas across the city. All of the visiting teams were transported to and from the games from their hotel by chartered buses. I had my headquarters in the Harbor Towers Hotel and the Victoria Amateur Radio Club provided the communications for the Host Committee (this was before cell phones).

Provinces and States represented in the tournament included: Ontario (three teams), Manitoba (two teams), Saskatchewan (seven teams), Alberta (twenty-one teams), Yukon (one team), British Columbia (fifteen teams), California (one team), Washington (one team), and Alaska (one team). We estimated that the number of players and fans (mostly spouses) that came with each team averaged about thirty, so the tournament brought into Victoria about 1,500 visitors for about a week, each spending at least $1,000 hence, bringing in over $1.5 million in business. Because of the success of the tournament, the United Commercial Travelers presented to me the Salesman of the Year award at their annual banquet and the Victoria Tourism Bureau gave me a citation in terms of their President Award.

I started the organization of the Third Annual Tournament but in December 1999 I handed the chairmanship over to Jack

Hennis due to work commitments with my new job as an Acting Director of the Inventory Branch of the B.C. Forest Service. Jack remained chairman for the next 25 years and the average number of teams that participated each year has been over 110.

I gradually eased out of hockey after the third annual tournament and focused on my career. But, Ken King, who was very active in the United Commercial Travelers of America (UCT), involved me in UCT and I became President (Senior Councilor) of the Victoria Chapter in 1984, the year that Ken became its International President (Supreme Councilor). Ken's inauguration was in the Grand Hotel, Las Vegas. Rose and I were part of the official ceremonies.

I was given the honor of accepting the banner of the Supreme Councilor on behalf of his home council of Victoria, Local 434. I was expected to wear white slacks and a blue shirt for the event. Unfortunately, I left the purchase of the slacks for the last minute and I could not get it fixed at the bottom. So I just took the pants with me to Las Vegas, hoping to get it done there. We arrived there on a Friday evening and I went for a run on the strip the next morning. There I saw a shop that offered services of mending cloths. I went back to the hotel, changed and took the pants with me. I went in the shop and asked if they could fix up the pants while I was waiting. The seamstress said that for urgent work I needed to talk to the owner. She went to get the owner, who was about my age, an attractive lady who looked familiar, as if I had met her before. After explaining to her my predicament, that I needed the pants for that evening, she agreed to have it done while I was waiting. She then asked for my name and I pronounced it in the English version, which sounds like Hedgyi.

She said, "Could you spell it please." I did.

She said, "Shame on you. That is not how this name is pronounced." She pronounced it correctly with a perfect Hungarian accent.

I was impressed and asked her, "How do you know the right pronunciation."

She replied in Hungarian: "Because my name is Hegyi."

After comparing notes, we realized that we were actually distant cousins. Small consolation as she still charged me the full amount for the work. This further confirmed that she was from my father's side of the family (the tough ones!).

In 1980, I moved from the 200 member Kiwanis Club of Victoria to help out a new club in our area, the Kiwanis Club of Gordon Head, which was below charter strength of the required twenty members. I was elected its President in 1981 on a platform that I would bring in new members. By the end of 1982, we built up membership to forty-five and had a lot of good projects in our community, including chartering a service club of students at the University of Victoria.

In 1984, I was elected Lt. Governor for Division 17, Pacific Northwest District, Kiwanis International. I received training in leadership and club administration by Chuck Clutts, the District Governor, and was required to attend District Board meetings that were held every three months, mostly in Washington and Oregon. My responsibilities included providing leadership training for club officers of ten Kiwanis Clubs in our area, visiting each club at least three times during the year to give motivational talks, and to promote the good work of Kiwanis. Since Kiwanis meetings included either lunch or dinner, depending on the clubs, and I was attending so many meetings, I started to put on weight.

After seeing my weight climb by 30 lbs., I joined the Nautilus Club in Victoria, and started attending aerobics classes. In less than a year, I lost 30 lbs. and was feeling very fit. This helped to keep my arthritis under control and, on Saturday mornings, I was able to attend *the super sweat* classes, which were lead by two instructors for an hour-and-a-half without a break. Now that I was associating with people who were committed to fitness, I was encouraged to start an annual fitness festival. We held the first one on March 9, 10, and 11, 1984. It involved thirteen different sports and over 1,000 athletes who were thirty years and older. The sports included in the festival were: aerobics, badminton, bowling, cycling, darts, ladies field hockey, orienteering, rugby, 10K run, slow pitch, soccer, tennis ranked and tennis open. We ran this event for five years and it turned out to be a good promoter of physical fitness.

I had the opportunity of co-producing two shows on Rogers's community TV (one in 1987 and another in 1988). Each show lasted twenty minutes and included an introduction of the sports festival by myself in an interview format, excerpts from events of the previous year, and a demonstration of an aerobics class by instructors, including myself. I was extremely happy with my physical condition, considering that fifteen years earlier I had been facing the possibility of spending the rest of my days in a wheelchair. Here I was keeping up with professional aerobics instructors on a TV show.

In 1985, I was appointed District Circle K Administrator, responsible for the Kiwanis sponsored youth organizations at the College level. The territory I was responsible for covered states of Oregon, Washington, Alaska and part of Idaho, as well as the Province of British Columbia. I enjoyed working with the college students who were eager to volunteer their time to help those less fortunate. While I was responsible for providing leadership training for the Lt. Governors and the District Governor, I tried to do this privately and let them be in charge in front of their peers. I was reappointed to this position for another three years until 1989. I consider this period to be the most rewarding experience in my life. It renewed my faith in the human race as I was working with those highly responsible and caring young men and women, realizing that they would be leaders in the future and would touch many lives in a positive manner.

In 1986, I was leading aerobics at Circle K District Board meetings and at their annual convention. They told me that they very much appreciated these sessions, especially since Circle K-ers have the tendency of thinking of Kiwanians as old men and women. In 1988, I was asked to hold an aerobic class at the International Convention in Miami. It was featured in the program, and the 7 a.m. class was attended by about fifty students. The following year I had to repeat this performance at the International Convention in St. Louis. For the previous two year's work, I was awarded by Circle K International with the *Distinguished Administrator* honor.

In 1990, I was elected Governor of the Pacific Northwest District, Kiwanis International. This was one of the largest districts in the Kiwanis organization. In that year, we had 440 clubs divided into forty-four Districts and a membership of approximately 10,000 active men and women dedicated to providing service in their community. Kiwanis International President, Dr. Wil Blechman, provided excellent training for all forty-six Governors, with the assistance of the staff at the international office. As District Governor, I was chairman of the board that consisted of forty-four Lt. Governors. I was responsible for coordinating their work, as well as the activities of twenty District committee chairs. Rose and I were required to make an official visit to each division or groups of them, to provide further training and to give motivational talks at official meetings and at banquets.

It was an incredible year. We traveled off Vancouver Island forty-four times, spending each weekend visiting divisions in the district and clubs. It was also a major commitment of time and money (it cost us over $30,000), but the opportunity of providing service and making friends was definitely worth it. It was my way of repaying a debt that I felt I owed to the many people who helped me since that night in the Salvation Army hostel.

As Governor, I always spoke from the heart without notes. Our theme was E.S.P. (Expand Service Potential) through the sponsored youth program. I am still very proud to have been part of the International Board that established a major emphasis program that has become the flagship of Kiwanis: *Children, Priority One*.

Journey to the Big World

Joining the Private Sector

In 1990, we completed the digital conversion of 7,320 forest cover maps. While introducing pioneering technology into a traditional government department was initially exciting and a lot of fun, the emergence of Information Systems Branches in the various Ministries slowed down the progress considerably. In the late 1980,s some of the Directors of the Information Systems Branches opted to exercise control over all operations that used computers. These Directors had difficulty in accepting the fact that computers were the new tools for Government Departments to do their business. The Director's role was to support such operations rather than to control them. The control that some of the ISB directors tried to put on the line department was about the biggest waste of tax payers money that I have seen in government. I personally did not want to waste my time with unproductive *turf* fighting. I decided to move into a more challenging work environment, the private sector.

Since I did not know much about the operations of a private sector company, I teamed up with Penny Walker, who was experienced with the procedures of the private sector. We formed a high tech company called Ferihill Technologies Ltd., on a 50-50 % ownership. I sold our house and invested a substantial amount of the proceeds into this company. As we needed operating funds, I cashed in my government pension to provide the financing. This was a painful thing to do because the government decided to withhold their matching contributions and then took my half for taxes. I still have a bone to pick with government about this.

By investing in a high tech company, I provided employment for about fifteen people. Some of my colleagues, who were forced to leave government because they were not up with technological developments, were given the golden handshake. I was determined to succeed. Accepting failure was not an option. When people questioned me about the wisdom of my decision, I replied, "Remember, when you eat bacon and egg for breakfast, it is the chicken who contributed, but the pig who made the commitment."

The first product that we developed was a data management system with electronic images for Corrections Canada. This was for the Admissions and Discharge Unit. As inmates were booked in, the Admissions and Discharge officer would take a digital image of them with a video camera. This was before the advent of digital cameras. We installed an image capture board into a PC then hooked up the video camera to it. We developed the software to grab the image as a .jpeg file and linked it to dbase3 data base Identification Cards could be printed for the inmates while they were inside the jail, as well as when they were released.

We extended this system to provide ID cards for all staff and support workers. I installed this system into twelve Correctional Institutions in Canada, including the maximum security correctional institute in Kent, British Columbia. Taking computer equipment into a correctional institute was quite a unique experience. Although I knew that I could come through the heavily guarded gates and security at any time, it was still a chilling feeling as I proceeded from one section to another, with the heavy metal doors slamming behind me and waiting until the next one opened to let me through.

We had to calibrate the system inside in terms of picture quality in an environment that did not have the best lighting conditions. Inmates were available to pose during the calibration. My daughter, Jennifer, came with me to do the training of the A/D staff and we both stayed after to help with the live bookings for a day at least. This was an intimidating experience. As we took the pictures of the inmates, many of them appeared friendly, but when we linked the data base, the criminal record of each inmate showed up, which included murder, break and entry, rape and child molestation. In addition, we witnessed some interesting episodes involving conversations among inmates about the length of their sentence, complaints about the quality of colour television and the inadequacy of recreational facilities.

The second product that we started to develop was a Mobile Technical Office (MTO) for resource management. This product facilitated the downloading of digital resource maps onto laptop computers, which were then connected to Global Positioning (GPS) and wireless data transmission systems to allow resource managers to view corporate data sets in the field, as well as to navigate to their work sites in a cost effective and safe way.

However, in 1993, I could see that the partnership was not working well, so we decided to split the company into two: Penny took the business associated with the imaging system, while I continued the development of the MTO product under a new name, Hegyi GeoTechnologies International Inc. (HGI).

MTO facilitated that digital forest cover maps, forest inventory and cruise data, electronic tally sheets and forms, digital air photos and all other aspects of the corporate database could be made available in the field on hand-held pen-based computers. We installed laptop computers with Global Positioning Systems (GPS) into Forest Service vehicles and connected them with the Ranger Station through wireless data transmission. Field personnel were able to see on the laptop computer in their vehicle where they were traveling, including tracking their journey on digital maps. This was especially useful in the bush where there were no road signs on logging roads and it was easy to get lost or disoriented. The safety aspect of this technology was also important. We designed the system so that field officers could automatically check in with the Ranger station every two hours by clicking on the "check in" icon on the laptop computer. The system sent to the computer at the Ranger Station or District Office time stamped GPS coordinate of each field officer.

A special feature of the MTO software was the capability of issuing violation notices and tickets. Previously, if a logging company was harvesting timber in a way that damaged the environment, such as the water system, the Field Officer had to get the District Manager (his/her supervisor) to issue a "stop work order". Previously this would take days for the District Manager to go back and find the logger. With our system, the Field Officer was able to write up the citation on the laptop computer, send the draft through wireless data transmission to his/her supervisor who would check it out and send back a "stop work order" ticket electronically with his/her signature on it. The Field Officer would then print the ticket on a portable printer and hand it to the representative of company who was doing the violation. This process could be completed in less than twenty minutes at a significant cost savings.

As a product, MTO became successful. Market penetration included B.C. government agencies, Alberta Department of Environment, Canadian Forestry Service, Ontario Ministry of Natural Resources, Environment Canada, U.S. Forest Service and private sector agencies. Internationally, MTO facilitated projects with CIDA and the Canadian Space agency, covering countries such as Brazil, Argentina, Hungary, and Russia.

Picture 30. Mobile Technical Office.

Because of the expanding international nature of the business, Rose and I decided to move to Ottawa in 1994 while maintaining the office in Victoria. We stayed in an apartment for three years just to make sure that we would want live in Ottawa.

After all, the climate in Victoria is much better and our move to Ottawa was viewed by some of our friends as being close to insanity. Once we finalized our decision, we decided to buy either a condo or a house. We were looking at condos on Kilborn Avenue, but it was obvious that Rose had enough of apartment living and wanted to get back to gardening.

As we left the condo building and returned to our car, Rose said, "I need to go to the washroom." Well, she didn't want to go back to the condo building, so I said that we could drive out to Bank Street and find a Café. The weather was quite miserable. it was raining and a bit cold. I made a wrong turn and found myself on a "No Exit" street where they were building new bungalows. I noticed the demo unit so I suggested to Rose, "Let's go in. You can use the washroom there."

She said, "Okay, but let's not make it too obvious. You talk to the salesperson while I find the washroom."

We walked and were greeted by a sales lady who introduced herself as Doreen. She asked: "May I help you?"

I replied, "Yes. Actually, my wife needs to use the washroom." Doreen responded with a big smile while Rose gave me a look before retreating to the washroom.

When Rose returned from the washroom, we walked around the house. She said to me, "This is exactly what I was looking for." She liked the high ceiling, open kitchen, finished basement, small garden in the back and three bathrooms!

I went up to Doreen and said, "My wife likes the bathroom, so we are interested in making an offer."

Doreen burst into laughter and said, "I have been selling houses for twenty years, and this is a new one." Since we had a pre-approved mortgage with the Royal Bank, we were able to buy the house the next day.

In 1997, Working Ventures invested $1 million in HGI to enhance the product development. In 1998, we opened an office in Hungary with the focus on developing software and hardware to reduce and prevent car theft. In 1999, I rented an apartment in Budapest and spent half of my time there leading the software development work.

In 1999, a Toronto-based company offered to buy HGI. They were lunching a company to offer services in the transportation industry for independent truckers. The intention was to provide an infrastructure between shippers and independent truckers to deliver goods to consignees. HGI was to supply Automatic Vehicle Location (AVL) hardware units in the trucks, equipped with GPS and wireless data transmission capabilities. HGI software in the Operations Centre would be able to show the movement of the independent trucking fleet on street level digital maps. The location of shippers would also be shown on these maps, as well as that of the major consignees. The targeted operations would involve the following steps:

- Shippers would post on the system electronically the requests to transport merchandize from their locations to designated consignees whose address would show up automatically on the digital maps.

- The locations of trucks registered with the system could then be shown relative to these requests. A truck which was closest to the location of a shipper that was requesting transportation service and had spare capacity could then bid on the job at a lower cost than those who were further away.

The new company was to offer this service for a fee. Business projections were rather bullish and, as a result, the HGI technology appeared to have a lucrative opportunity.

After due diligence was completed, the sale of HGI to the Toronto-based company occurred. The payment for HGI was offered in terms of shares in the new company that was to own HGI and it was going for IPO with about $26 million investment from Bay Street. The value of my shares in this new company was estimated to be approximately $2 million. The idea was that I would stay with HGI for a year as its CEO, after which I could start selling my shares and plan my retirement. I felt that I had met my goal of becoming a millionaire within ten years.

In the fall of 1999, HGI won a contract with the U.S. Law Enforcement Task Force, coordinated by the Minneapolis Police Department, to develop an integrated hardware and software system for bait and covert applications. I decided to develop the hardware units and the software programs in Hungary. I leased an apartment in Budapest and was trying to get used to the Hungarian lifestyles.

Life in Hungary ten years after the fall of Communism was most interesting. Some of the people who were not entrepreneurial, including my sister, felt that they had been better off under Communism. They had jobs, a roof over their heads and enough food to enjoy life. They were protected by the State. Entrepreneurs, on the other hand, were going full steam ahead to make up for time lost under Communism. The population in general enjoyed the new freedom and opportunities. Items in stores were abundant and the free enterprise spirit of the go-getters was showing its rewards in terms of beautiful homes, top of the line cars and dining in restaurants with impressive wine consumptions.

    The system that we designed for bait cars consisted of a hardware unit with GPS and wireless data transmission modems and a programmable microprocessor. This unit had input/output connections to car doors, battery, horn, engine starter and trunk hood. The unit was hidden in the trunk of a bait car, which was a car that police placed at a strategic location where thieves would go and take it. However, when the thieves opened the door, our unit would sense it and the microprocessor would activate the GPS and the wireless data transmission modem, send a message to our monitoring software that was installed at the 911 centre, indicating the car's location on a street level map where the thieves were driving the car. A police car would then be dispatched to catch the thieves and, once the police was in eye contact with the car, they could disable its engine and lock the doors. In cases when the stolen car was hidden in a garage or building, the police were able to activate the horn of the stolen car through a cell phone in order to find out where the thieves were hiding the car. I was in charge of the development of this system and it was a great feeling of accomplishment when the acceptance of the system was signed off by the police.

However, the fall of the .com companies resulted in cold feet by the Bay Street investors and the transportation company that I had shares in did not go for IPO. Hence, the shares that I had received for HGI came down in value from $2million to $0. This experience taught me an important lesson about corporate acquisitions. The company that had purchased HGI was able to *acquire* the IP of HGI and market it through another company that started to operate under a *shell* that was listed on the Toronto stock exchange. They became the beneficiary of my investment and hard work, a lesson well learned and I am happy that this experience left me without any feelings of bitterness.

I had been too focused on technology development and had not paid enough attention to the tricky legal maneuverings. Therefore, I was the one who had to take responsibility for this costly slip up. In August 2001, I resigned my position with HGI, and decided to start all over again in my desire to become a millionaire. As the saying goes, *I gave up on my first million. I am now working on the second!*

I resumed the international circuit with a focus on business development in India. The Canadian International Development Agency (CIDA INC) provided financial contributions towards these efforts. We also received moral support from the Department of Foreign Affairs and International Trade (DFAIT) through a high profile trade delegation.

During my visit to India, I looked for an Indian company with whom I could establish a business alliance for the purpose of transferring our Emergency Preparedness and Disaster Management technology to India. During the New Delhi stop, I

Journey to the Big World

was introduced to Mr. Asok Mookerjee, Managing Director of Lea Associates South Asia (LASA), a highly successful civil engineering company with Canadian routes. Randy Trenholm, Manager of the India desk of CIDA INC (Canadian International Development Agency, Industry partnership program), suggested that we play a game of golf with Asok in New Delhi. In Canada, I was just starting to play golf so I was a bit reluctant to accept Randy's suggestion. But, according to Randy, the establishment of personal trust and friendship is an important ingredient of business relationship in India.

We arranged a game with Asok for Saturday April 27th. I was to fly out that night. I checked out of my room in the Hotel Sheraton in the morning, put my luggage in Randy's room and Asok picked us up in a chauffeur-driven car at 9:00 a.m. We teed off time was at 10:00 a.m. at Jaypee Greens Private Club in Noida, north-west outskirt of New Delhi. I was partnered with the former Director General in the Ministry of Highways and Randy played with Asok. Asok had borrowed two extra sets of clubs for Randy and I. Randy was left handed and he had to play with right handed clubs. I decided that I was not looking too badly in comparison to him. We had two power carts and each of us had a caddy to carry our clubs and find the balls. We played eighteen holes of very enjoyable golf in temperatures of almost 40°C.

Picture 31. Delegation to India with the Canadian Energy Minister.

After the game, we went into the Clubhouse and had local King Fisher beer and a light snack. It was a good opportunity to talk business. It encouraged me to want to meet with Asok on my next trip to India. (Asok and I have become very good friends and trusted business associates since that game).

Asok then drove us back to the hotel. I changed quickly and rented a hotel limousine to take me to the airport. Unfortunately, I had booked to traveled in Economy Class. My flight was leaving at midnight and it was 9 p.m. when I got to the airport, assuming that three hours would be enough time to check in. When we arrived at the airport, the driver inquired which line I should join. He told me that the lines were so long that it was estimated to take over two hours just to get into the building. I offered him a good tip to help me find a quicker alternative. He had a porter friend who specialized in these things, and they told me that $40 US would get me into the Business Class counter in fifteen minutes. They had connections there and they would accept my Economy Class ticket to issue a boarding pass. I did that and I was inside security in less than half an hour.

I continued with golf and managed to improve my score from 120 (eighteen holes) from the time I first played in New Delhi to ninety holes. My son, Michael, and I play a game each time I visit him in Madison and also whenever he visits Ottawa. Also, when Asok comes to Ottawa to do business, I always line up a couple of games for him. He does the same when I go to India. Since 2002, I have made fourteen trips to India on business. Asok and I have managed to squeeze in a couple of games during each visit.

Picture 32. Golfing in India with Asok (with hat) and Randy Trenholm (seated).

Life has been good, I enjoyed the places we visited. My children all have successful careers and Rose and I have a good life. I am still working and I am truly happy.

Conclusion

I have been successful in Government and in the private sector. I was happy in Government and in the private sector. I have loved my travels and the people that I have met. I travelled around the world and secured many friends.

Nagy Papa, rest in peace. I have lived the life you talked about in your stories, I have ventured out into the *big world,* and I have loved it.

Picture 33. My Grandfather (Nagy Papa)

www.ingramcontent.com/pod-product-compliance
Lightning Source LLC
Chambersburg PA
CBHW061301110426
42742CB00012BA/2016